$\mathcal{A}H$

5G Form Prize

Presented to

Edward Millett

Prize Giving

2004

N M

Headmaster

ARNOLD HOUSE SCHOOL

SWEET CHARIOT

THE COMPLETE BOOK OF THE RUGBY WORLD CUP

2003

WITH CONTRIBUTIONS FROM

Rob Andrew

Eddie Butler

Gareth Chilcott

Mick Cleary

Terry Cooper

Jill Douglas

Brendan Gallagher

Alastair Hignell

John Inverdale

Chris Jones

Stephen Jones

Jim Neilly

SWEET CHARIOT

THE COMPLETE BOOK OF THE RUGBY WORLD CUP

2003

EDITOR
Ian Robertson

MAINSTREAM
PUBLISHING

in association with

Scottish Life
a marketing division of Royal London

First published in Great Britain in 2003 by
MAINSTREAM PUBLISHING COMPANY (EDINBURGH) LTD
7 Albany Street
Edinburgh EH1 3UG

ISBN 1 84018 822 7

From rugby to racing –
editor Ian Robertson enjoys
Melbourne Cup day with
contributors Jill Douglas and
John Inverdale, and BBC
colleague Alison Rusted

Produced by Lennard Books
A division of Lennard Associates Limited
Mackerye End, Harpenden, Herts, AL5 5DR

Production editor: Chris Marshall
Text and cover design: Paul Cooper Design

Printed and bound in Great Britain by
CPI Bath

ACKNOWLEDGEMENTS

The publishers would like to thank Dave Rogers, Adam Pretty,
Nick Laham, Chris McGrath, Daniel Berehulak, Mark Nolan,
Sean Garnsworthy, Hamish Blair, Mark Dadswell, Rob Cianflone,
Tony Lewis, Darren England, Jonathan Wood, Jon Buckle, Ryan Pierse,
Stuart Hannagan, Cameron Spencer, Mark Kolbe of the Getty Images team
and also the Getty Images/AFP photographers who provided such excellent
photographic coverage of Rugby World Cup 2003.

Thanks also to Matt Homes and Justin Davies in the
Getty Images London office for their editorial support,
and to Clare Robertson for her secretarial back-up.

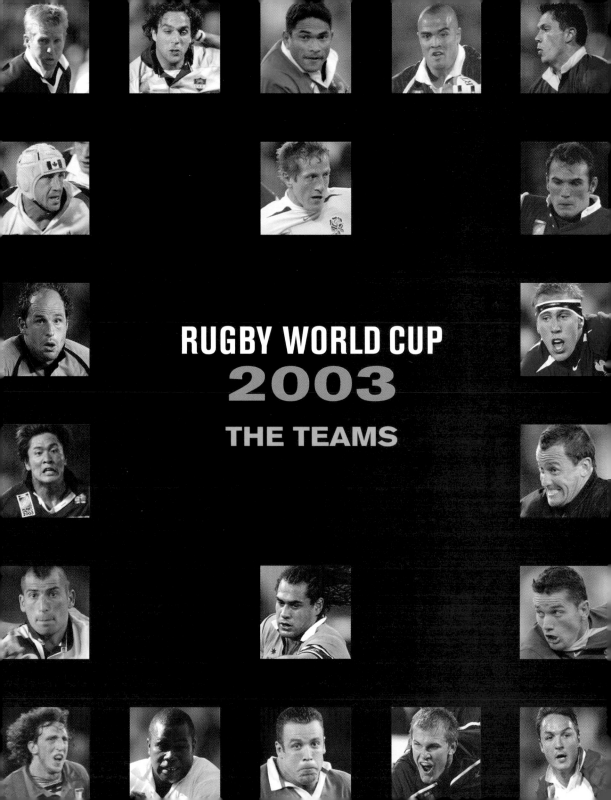

RUGBY WORLD CUP
2003
THE TEAMS

U.S.A

Rugby team

SOUTH AFRICA

Rugby team

ARGENTINA

Rugby team

Never underestimate the importance of local knowledge.

A rugby fan understands which team each animal represents. It's this sort of "insider" knowledge that HSBC values.

At HSBC, we have banks in more countries than anyone else. And each one is staffed by local people.

We have offices in 79 countries and territories; Europe, Asia-Pacific, the Americas, the Middle East, and Africa.

Being local enables them to offer insights into financial opportunities and create service initiatives that would never occur to an outsider.

It means our customers get the kind of local knowledge and personal service that you'd expect of a local bank. And a level of global knowledge and widely sourced expertise that you wouldn't.

The world's local bank

Issued by HSBC Holdings plc.

Contents

Introduction

11   The Greatest Show on Turf – ALASTAIR HIGNELL

The Pools

21   **POOL A**
The Gold and the Green – JIM NEILLY

35   **POOL B**
Les Bleus Rule the Roost – JILL DOUGLAS

49   **POOL C**
England Weather Southern Storms – MICK CLEARY

63   **POOL D**
Black Tide Advancing – STEPHEN JONES

Quarter-Finals

77   New Zealand v South Africa – BRENDAN GALLAGHER

89   Australia v Scotland – JILL DOUGLAS

101   France v Ireland – JIM NEILLY

113   England v Wales – MICK CLEARY

Semi-Finals

125   New Zealand v Australia – STEPHEN JONES

135   France v England – MICK CLEARY

Third-Place Play-Off

145   New Zealand v France – ALASTAIR HIGNELL

The Final

153   Australia v England – JOHN INVERDALE

Retrospective

173   Looking Back – ALASTAIR HIGNELL

Highlights

177   Player of the Tournament: Jonny Wilkinson –
EDDIE BUTLER

179   Rugby World Cup 2003: World XV –
ROB ANDREW & GARETH CHILCOTT

183   The Highs and the Lows – CHRIS JONES

187   **Statistics**

foreword

Scottish Life's involvement with rugby – at international, club and youth levels – goes back over many years. So I am delighted that Scottish Life has been able to support the production of this book to celebrate the fifth Rugby World Cup.

The Rugby World Cup has become a major international sporting event and the 2003 event provided some truly wonderful examples of sporting endeavour and skill at their very best. It also provided some classic moments of drama and excitement – and not only from matches involving the traditional 'top' teams.

Although we are a Scottish business, we salute the winners, England, and acknowledge the joy and pride that their victory brings to so many of our customers. But we are also indebted to all the national sides who provided a feast of top-class rugby, lasting over six weeks.

This book provides a great record of the action, the detail, the colour and the passion of the 2003 Rugby World Cup. I am proud that Scottish Life is associated with it and I am sure that as a rugby fan, you will enjoy it as a lasting record of a great tournament.

Brian Duffin

Chief Executive

Scottish Life

+ 44 (0)20 8410 8444   www.landrover.com   Drive responsibly off-road

BUILT TO TACKLE ANYTHING Official sponsor of England Rugby.

THE LAND ROVER EXPERIENCE

INTRODUCTION
The Greatest Show on Turf

ALASTAIR HIGNELL

'Just like the Olympics, only bigger!' The prediction of the Channel Seven weather forecaster may have been based more on the desire to gain brownie points from his employer – host broadcaster for Rugby World Cup 2003 – than on any concern for statistical accuracy, but to many Australians it rang very true. Whereas the 2000 Olympiad had been based more or less in Sydney and had been over and done with in fourteen days, rugby's fifth global tournament was aimed at the whole of Australia and was going to last just over seven weeks. Australians

ABOVE **Sydney gets in the spirit ahead of Rugby World Cup 2003 with a giant rugby ball, accompanied by fireworks, illuminating the Harbour Bridge. Sydney provided two venues for RWC 2003 – Aussie Stadium and Telstra Stadium, the former Stadium Australia.**

had been rightly proud of the way they had staged the world's biggest sporting event three years previously, and now they were confident of putting on a show that would be every bit as well run, as spectacular and as successful.

ABOVE **The teams arrive. Ireland's Keith Wood autographs shirts after landing at Sydney. The hosts went to great lengths to make the participants feel welcome and urged locals to be generous in their support of less powerful sides such as Romania and Namibia.**

'The greatest show on turf', featuring 48 matches at 11 venues in 10 cities, was set to break all records. The opening match, at Telstra Stadium (previously Stadium Australia), Sydney, was guaranteed to exceed the top attendance figure for a World Cup match. Seventy-five thousand had watched the England v South Africa quarter-final in Paris in 1999. Telstra Stadium – venue not just for the opening match and the final but also for both semi-finals, the third-place play-off and two other matches – seats 83,500. With huge, well-appointed rugby league and Australian Rules stadia being pressed into service as well, the previous record for a World Cup match in Australia – 22,000 saw Australia play France at Sydney's Concord Oval in the semi-final of the first World Cup in 1987 – was about to be eclipsed many times over.

A record number of bums on seats – the organisers reckoned that two million people would watch the matches at the grounds – was to be matched by a record number of couch potatoes. With more than 200 countries taking television feeds, according to the IRB, the estimated television reach was set to top four billion. In 1999 it had been 3.1 billion. Back in 1987, with only 17 countries taking pictures, it had been 180 million.

One of the big reasons for the increase in paying spectators was that – not by design – Rugby World Cup 2003 was to be played in one country. It was fully intended that the tournament would be shared, as in 1987, between Australia and New Zealand, with the latter, having staged the first final, taking on the role of sub host union. But when the New Zealand Rugby Union failed to guarantee 'clean' stadia, the International Rugby Board (IRB) felt it had no option other than to offer the tournament as a whole to Australia.

Brimming over with confidence following the success of the Sydney Olympics, the Australians embraced Rugby World Cup wholeheartedly. Thousands of volunteers signed up at all the

but also to learn and sing Georgian folksongs. The people of Launceston, Tasmania, were urged to side with either Namibia or Romania, the participants in the first ever rugby international on the island. Inhabitants born on even days of the month were expected to support one side, while those born on the odd days of the month were encouraged to get behind the other. Meanwhile, the government of South Australia officially renamed Kangaroo Island as Wallaby Island, and Australian patriotic fervour was further whipped up by the furore surrounding the International Rugby Board's decision to ban the official singing of 'Waltzing Matilda' before the Wallabies' matches.

Of all the 20 nations participating in the tournament, Namibia had taken perhaps the longest and toughest road. After beating Madagascar and Zimbabwe in the southern section of the African qualifying group, they faced Tunisia in a home-and-away play-off, and, after finishing level on aggregate points, scrambled through on the basis of tries scored. Georgia qualified for the World Cup

LEFT **Rugby mania strikes Oz. Keeper Corey Mead of the Australian Reptile Park gives Eric his 57th birthday present, a chocolate cake in the shape of an RWC 2003 ball. Eric, a 700kg saltwater crocodile, did not wait for the cake to be sliced.**
BELOW **Georgia front-row forward Goderdzi Shvelidze (right) worships with team-mates at the Russian Orthodox Church in Perth. Western Australians took a shine to the Georgians, whose union is in such financial straits that the IRB provided the team's kit.**

major venues. Events were planned to coincide with all the big matches, as the different host cities competed with each other to provide the warmest welcome. The public was encouraged to get behind the smaller teams, with a host of novel ideas designed to increase spectator participation. World Cup new boys Georgia, for instance, were adopted by Clancy's Fish Bar in Perth, which became their unofficial headquarters in the city, with customers encouraged not only to parade themselves in Georgian colours

for the first time, coming second to Ireland in their European group but gaining direct passage to Australia on the back of a gruelling 17-13 victory over ancient enemies Russia. The United States and Tonga qualified through the repechage system – the former through two 50-point victories over Spain, the latter scoring nearly 200 points in two one-sided victories over Korea.

Like Namibia, Uruguay were playing in only their second World Cup. Los Teros also did it the hard way, losing their first three qualifying games before bouncing back to snatch second place in the Americas group from the Eagles. Samoa, the most celebrated giant-killers in World Cup history after their 1991 success (as Western Samoa) against Wales, also struggled to qualify, finishing second in the Oceania group behind Fiji. Romania also got through as runners-up, finishing behind Italy but ahead of Spain in their group. World Cup regulars Canada (quarter-finalists in 1991), Fiji (who reached the last eight in the first tournament in 1987), Japan and Italy all cruised through their qualifying groups to book their appearances in Australia.

Those 12 teams had to work their passage to rugby's fifth World Cup, yet by the time the tournament kicked off, one of them was ranked third in the world – ahead, even, of reigning champions Australia. Ireland, under coach Eddie O'Sullivan, had strung together a sequence of 15 wins in 17 matches leading up to the World Cup, had beaten the Wallabies in Dublin and contested a Six Nations Grand Slam with England. The Wallabies, meanwhile, had had a disappointing Tri-Nations, with just the one narrow win over South Africa, and had lost six of their past ten matches. But the Wallabies were the only team to have won the World Cup twice, were the reigning champions and were playing on home soil. The bookies were not alone in reckoning Australia had a far better chance than Ireland of coming out on top at Telstra Stadium at the end of November.

By common consent, there were five teams with a good chance of being crowned world champions. France, like Australia and New Zealand, had appeared in two previous finals but, like the Wallabies, had displayed indifferent form in the run-in to the tournament. After winning the Grand Slam in 2002 and being named as the international team of the year, Les Bleus came unstuck in the 2003 Six Nations Championship, then lost two

Tests in Argentina and one in Australia. But they did beat England in Marseilles, and as the winners of the two most exciting World Cup matches of all time – last-four victories over Australia in 1987 and New Zealand in 1999 – France were being discounted by no one, especially England, who were scheduled to play Bernard Laporte's team in the semi-finals.

England were rated number one in the world by the IRB and were co-favourites with New Zealand in the eyes of the bookies. In ten matches leading up to the tournament, England had lost only once, when a second-string side went down to France in Marseilles by a single point, and had achieved a Six Nations Grand Slam, as well as winning in New Zealand and, for the first time in their history, in Australia – on successive weekends. Clive

LEFT **Sean Furter of Namibia wins line-out ball against Argentina. The Weltwitschias had a tough ride through qualifying, then found themselves in a pool with the Pumas, the Irish and the Wallabies.** RIGHT **The metronomic goal-kicking of Jonny Wilkinson was a significant weapon in the arsenal of England, who were rated number one in the world by the IRB at the start of the tournament.**

Woodward's men wanted for nothing in terms of resources and preparation and had form, experience and the world's best goal-kicker, Jonny Wilkinson, on their side. Woodward had appeared to have backed himself into a corner when he asked to be judged on England's World Cup results, only for his team to crash out of the 1999 tournament at the quarter-final stage. Now was the time for Martin Johnson and his team to stand and deliver.

First, though, they would have to get past the Springboks. South Africa had been excluded from the first two tournaments for political reasons but had won the third in their own country and had only ever lost one World Cup match – after extra time in a Twickenham semi-final to the eventual 1999 winners, Australia. Like Australia's, their Tri-Nations season had been disappointing and included just one victory. On top of that a race row engulfed the squad in controversy just weeks before they left South Africa, while injuries deprived them of a whole succession of key players. Yet their coach, Rudi Straeuli, and their veteran scrum half, Joost van der Westhuizen, knew what it was like to win a World Cup, and no one was writing them off.

But no one was betting too heavily against the All Blacks either. New Zealand had won the inaugural tournament, in 1987, and been favourites for every World Cup since. In 1991 they had been undone at the semi-final stage by a David Campese-inspired Australia. In 1995, despite the presence of Jonah Lomu, they had lost the final to a Nelson Mandela-inspired South Africa.

In 1999 the whole French team was inspired to overwhelm the favourites. Now, going in to the 2003 tournament, the All Blacks were on top form, having regained the Bledisloe Cup and blitzed both Australia and South Africa in the Tri-Nations.

The team that were victorious at Telstra Stadium on 22 November would not only have triumphed over the most open field in the tournament's history but would also have survived the greatest demands yet made on a squad of players. According to the IRB experts, the ball would be in play for longer – up by a staggering 50 per cent on earlier tournaments; the matches would last longer – with a playing time of at least 90 minutes (compared with 84 minutes in the 1991 tournament); and the average match in Rugby World Cup 2003 could expect to see something in the region of 260 passes, 130 rucks and mauls, 60 kicks in open play, over 6 tries and 64 points, as well as 10 replacements.

Fans at RWC 2003 could therefore expect a feast of entertainment once the rugby started, while the organisers, anticipating with relish the $800 million boost to the economy that 40,000 visitors would bring, made sure that even before the tournament kicked off there would be an opening ceremony to remember. Under the direction of Adelaide-born Andrew Walsh, a 2,000-strong cast produced an hour-long extravaganza of music, dance and movement, with one highlight a brilliantly choreographed sequence which produced an aerial view of a giant rugby player, represented by hundreds of card-waving dancers, that appeared to stride up the stadium and score a try.

Even though the firework finale had to be abandoned because of a rogue helicopter, the ceremony more than met its objectives. Walsh hoped that it would inspire, convey messages of joy, culture and friendship and set the tone for the tournament. On that basis fans at the greatest event of the year, and the third most important in the sporting calendar, were entitled to expect a riot of colour, an orgy of friendship and a feast of fast-moving and spectacular action.

FACING PAGE **Doug Howlett (left) and Kees Meeuws admire their likenesses on an All Blacks supporters' banner. But would they get their hands on the Webb Ellis Cup come 22 November?**
BELOW **Rocky the 'human animation' powers his way to the line during the opening ceremony, propelled by over 700 pairs of legs.**

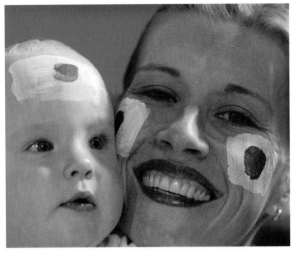

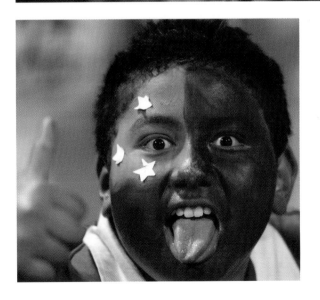

SUBMERGE YOURSELF

Delta is the No 1 US carrier across the Atlantic Ocean. With daily flights from London

INTO AN UNFORGETTABLE

Gatwick to Atlanta and Cincinnati, as well as, Manchester to Atlanta, and onward connections

HOLIDAY.

to 170 US cities, let Delta take you where you want to go.

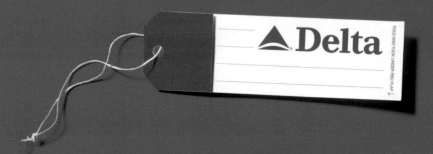

Sunshine, water sports, amusement parks and lots more fun are waiting for you.

For more information on Delta log on to www.delta.com or call reservations on 0800 414 767.

POOL A
The Gold and the Green

JIM NEILLY

J ust in case it could be interpreted as the opening line to a convoluted Irish joke, the build-up to Ireland's World Cup really did begin in Western Siberia 13 months before the squad left for Sydney. Having gone out of the 1999 tournament to Argentina on a black night in Lens, the Irish had to qualify and were drawn with Russia and Georgia, neither of whom were to present Eddie O'Sullivan's side with any serious problems.

Romania did, however, give Ireland some anxious moments in Limerick in a warm-up game, before Ireland came through 39-8 in the first international to be played at Thomond Park in

BELOW **George Smith walks on air. The Wallaby flanker gathers in at the line out in the memorable clash with Ireland at Telstra Dome, Melbourne. Australia prevailed, just, 17-16.**

2003

over 100 years. Then it was a trip into the unknown for the squad plus a handful of IRFU officials, the usual hardened press representatives and a group of enthusiastic, if somewhat bewildered, supporters, who boarded a charter flight to Moscow and then to Krasnoyarsk, the mid-point for the Trans-Siberian, Trans-Mongolian and Trans-Manchurian rail lines.

The Irish pronunciation of Krasnoyarsk, some 64 hours east of Moscow by train, can only be imagined, and, for a handful of the supporters, memories of an eventful weekend were made all the more evocative by the purchase of plastic 'campaign medals' which had to be worn at all times. A member of the Limerick contingent remarked, as he pinned another addition to his chest, 'One more of these, lads, and I qualify for a state pension!'

In a dilapidated football stadium, Ireland, led by Keith Wood, overcame a physical Russian challenge to win 35-3, but it was to be the last game for Ireland's talismanic captain for over a year. Wood was to miss 12 successive Tests following surgery for a serious shoulder injury and a protracted spell of recovery and rehabilitation.

If Wood's absence was a major blow, the Irish made light of it, and having seen off Georgia 63-14 at Lansdowne Road to secure their place in the 2003 World Cup finals, they had a month to prepare for three November Tests, two of which were against sides whom they would face a year later in Australia.

On a filthy Dublin day, Ireland swarmed all over Australia, the reigning world champions, and as a rampant Irish forward pack took the honours, Ronan O'Gara kicked six penalties for an 18-9 victory, the first in 12 Tests between the countries and a first win for Ireland in 23 years. Brian O'Driscoll, the youngest player in the Ireland side, had retained the captaincy after the win against Georgia. Following the victory over the Wallabies, he steered Ireland to a 64-17 defeat of Fiji eight days later, and, significantly, to a win over Argentina 18-9 which helped, in no small measure, to expunge the nightmare of Lens three years earlier.

O'Driscoll was to remain as Ireland's captain throughout the 2003 Six Nations Championship, which saw Ireland cruise past Scotland at Murrayfield by 36-6, followed just six days later by a win against Italy in Rome by 37-13, with O'Driscoll scoring his 18th international try to pass Brendan Mullin's Irish record (now held by Denis Hickie). Things got a lot harder, with Ireland squeezing past France in Dublin 15-12 thanks to a Geordan Murphy dropped goal and four David Humphreys penalties, the

Ulster out-half having established himself once again following an injury to Ronan O'Gara, who had been at the helm against Australia and Argentina the previous autumn.

However, it was O'Gara's injury-time dropped goal that snatched victory by 25-24 for an exhausted Irish team in Cardiff, but hopes of a first Irish Grand Slam in 55 years were buried by an irresistible England, who demolished Ireland in Dublin 42-6 to take the prize that had eluded them in the previous four seasons.

A depleted squad travelled to the southern hemisphere in June 2003 and showed signs of fatigue after a long season, going down to Australia 45-16 in Perth. Most of the first-choice players returned home after that match, but led by Reggie Corrigan – who had taken over from David Humphreys, in charge against Australia – Ireland defeated Tonga 40-19 in Nuku'alofa and Samoa 40-14 in Apia, with Ronan O'Gara's 32 points against the Samoans setting a new Irish record in an international.

RIGHT **Australia's former rugby league star winger Wendell Sailor opens the try account for RWC 2003 in the 20th minute of the Wallabies' encounter with Argentina at Sydney's Telstra Stadium.**

Ireland's World Cup preparations began in earnest with games against familiar Six Nations opposition, and with Keith Wood back in harness Ireland looked impressive, beating Wales 35-12 in Dublin, Italy 61-6 in Limerick and Scotland 29-10 at Murrayfield. The Italian and Scots wins were marred by injuries to Rob Henderson and, more seriously, to Geordan Murphy, who suffered a badly broken leg against the Scots, depriving Ireland and the World Cup of a glorious talent.

Eddie O'Sullivan's 30-man selection provoked considerable controversy, with the most notable omissions being flankers David Wallace and Kieron Dawson and lock Leo Cullen, who had played in 14 of the 17 games prior to the World Cup. Ulster centre Jonny Bell, a member of the 1995 and 1999 squads, was a late withdrawal, but the return to fitness of wing Shane Horgan, who had missed ten games, and prop John Hayes, missing for six, brought considerable relief.

After a week in Portugal, the squad returned to Dublin, where, on successive evenings, explorer Sir Ranulph Fiennes and former world middleweight boxing champion Marvin Hagler provided contrasting insights into achievement at the highest level. Hagler, who had been flown from Milan, his home for many years, was a particular favourite since many of the squad had more than a passing interest in boxing. One player offered the gem, 'If we get lost in Australia, at least we'll be able to fight our way out!'

Based for the first three weeks of the tournament in Terrigal, at the heart of the Central Coast region, Ireland revelled in excellent weather and five-star accommodation, in the knowledge that a sequence of Romania, Namibia, Argentina and finally Australia was as good as they would have wished for in what had been dubbed 'The Group of Death'.

As the Irish enjoyed outstanding training facilities at the local grammar school, regular golf outings and even a trip to Sydney to

2008

visit the set of television soap *Home and Away*, the spectre of the rematch with Argentina was all too evident, and successive press briefings accentuated the desire for revenge over the Pumas, who had beaten France twice and had come within a whisker of victory against South Africa a few months earlier.

The tournament's opening game held more than a passing interest for Ireland, as defending champions Australia and Argentina met, after a spectacular opening ceremony, in front of more than 80,000 spectators in Sydney's Telstra Stadium. Eddie O'Sullivan noted the inefficiency of the Pumas' line out, Felipe Contepomi's shortcomings as a goal-kicker and also the ominous ease with which the Wallabies went about securing a vital win, denying Argentina a bonus point in the process. Australia, with tries from Wendell Sailor and Joe Roff plus a conversion and four penalties from Elton Flatley, won 24-8, giving notice that they had no intention of relinquishing their hold on the Webb Ellis trophy, which they refer to, with typical Australian candour, as 'Bill'!

Gosford's picturesque Central Coast Stadium provided the venue for Ireland's opening game, and a capacity crowd in the region of 20,000 saw Ireland despatch Romania 45-17. Irish out-half David Humphreys made light of a gale-force wind, kicking three early penalties and converting tries by Shane Horgan, back in action after ten months of inactivity, and Keith Wood, who took a lovely pass from Peter Stringer to gallop in from 30 metres. Another Humphreys penalty gave the Ulsterman 16 points, and Ireland turned round 26-0 up and in seemingly commanding form.

Eddie O'Sullivan wasn't quite so happy about Ireland's second-half display, and while two tries by Denis Hickie and one by Victor Costello guaranteed a bonus point, Romania, showing huge commitment at the set pieces and in the tackle, scored 17 points to Ireland's 19 after the break. Ireland, able to use all seven replacements, including prop John Hayes for the first time in six months, lost No. 8 Anthony Foley with a knee injury that was to keep him sidelined for the next two matches.

Enter the part-timers from Namibia. Boasting only a handful of professionals who played with lesser South African provinces, the Namibian squad was composed of doctors, farmers, teachers, businessmen and even a lion tamer. Strictly speaking, flamboyant flanker Schalk van der Merwe, who made a 300-kilometre round trip twice a week to train in Windhoek, ran an animal sanctuary, but the press corps and assorted commentary teams couldn't resist the inference.

LEFT **Ireland's leading try scorer in internationals Denis Hickie crosses in the corner against Namibia on a rainsoaked evening in Sydney. Ireland scored ten tries to Namibia's one in a 64-7 win.**

Unhappy that his side had to play again just four days after the game with Australia, Pumas' coach Marcelo Loffreda made 14 changes to his starting line-up. Despite a try late in each half by Namibia, Argentina romped home 67-14 with ten tries, which included two penalty tries following ferocious forward pressure at five-metre scrums and two scores from pushovers – No. 8 Pablo Bouza touching down – to emphasise Argentina's appetite for set-piece play. With conditions in Gosford just about perfect for goal-kicking, Gonzalo Quesada, who looked much more assured than Felipe Contepomi had been against Australia, landed seven conversions and a penalty to ensure that he was going to claim the out-half position for the game against Ireland 12 days later.

The Australian coach, Eddie Jones, in total contrast to Loffreda, made only one change for the Wallabies' game with Romania in Brisbane, Daniel Vickerman coming in at lock for David Giffin, who was stretchered off against Argentina after a heavy fall. Fortunately, Giffin suffered only concussion and was to miss only one game. Meanwhile, his colleagues thrashed the Romanians 90-8 in a 13-try romp, the first coming after just 18 seconds when Elton Flatley, who went on to score 30 points, sliced through a bemused Romanian defence. Wallaby full back Mat Rogers, one of a handful of rugby league converts, scored a hat-trick, and Eddie Jones, who had been under constant pressure from the Australian press for his selections, was able to give all his replacements a run-out.

For Ireland's second game, against Namibia in Sydney's Aussie Stadium, Eddie O'Sullivan replaced David Humphreys with Ronan O'Gara, who had come off the bench against Romania, in the only change in the back division. In the forwards, though, John Hayes was in from the start at tight-head and O'Sullivan named a totally changed back row. Anthony Foley was ruled out, but a combination of Simon Easterby, Alan Quinlan and Eric Miller was indicative of O'Sullivan's dilemma regarding his best breakaway trio.

Quinlan, first capped as a replacement in the 1999 World Cup, scored the first of Ireland's ten tries after just three minutes, and by half-time Ireland had the game and a bonus point in the bag. Girvan Dempsey followed Quinlan onto the scoresheet, extending his Irish try-scoring record for a full back to eleven, and his Leinster colleague Denis Hickie then scored, making it eight tries in four games to take his overall Irish record to twenty-three. Prop forward Marcus Horan nabbed his first score at Test level after the video referee was consulted, and Eric Miller, displaying something like the form that had won him a Lions tour place in 1997, went over under the Namibian posts in a pretty fair impression of Brian O'Driscoll, leaving Namibian defenders grasping thin air as he sidestepped and dummied his way over from 20 metres out.

A sole Namibian try in the first half brought thunderous applause, but Ireland romped home with further tries from Quinlan and Miller, and one apiece from Shane Horgan and replacements Guy Easterby and John Kelly. Ronan O'Gara kicked seven conversions in dreadful conditions, and had the game not been played in a downpour from start to finish, Ireland would have gone well past the century, an ignominious statistic that the ill-matched Namibians were to be spared for only six days.

Ireland's victory was temporarily soured when the outspoken Namibian coach Dave Waterston, who had assisted Kitch Christie with South Africa in 1995 and had coached Tonga in 1999, cited Ireland's Paul O'Connell for stamping. The referee, Andrew Cole from Australia, had penalised O'Connell at the time, following consultation with his touch judge and fellow countryman Stuart Dickinson, but decided against a ten-minute sin-binning, or worse, for the big Irish lock, who was developing into one of the stars of the tournament.

Citing commissioner Dougie Hunter from Scotland decided immediately that there was no case to answer, but this information was withheld from the Irish management until 24 hours after the game had finished, leaving Ireland sweating on the outcome, knowing that a suspended player couldn't be replaced. Ulster's Gary Longwell had been on the injured list from just after the Irish arrival in Australia, and Leo Cullen, the stand-by lock, had dislocated his shoulder at home in a Celtic League fixture with Leinster, so Ireland were, at one stage, facing the prospect of just two fit locks in Malcolm O'Kelly and Donncha O'Callaghan.

Happily for Ireland, O'Connell escaped further censure, and the much-awaited rematch with Argentina grew closer and more relevant as the Pumas, with nine changes from the Namibian game, won comfortably at Aussie Stadium against the Romanians, notching up seven tries in a 50-3 victory. By that stage Marcelo Loffreda, the Pumas' coach, had used all thirty players over three games, keeping Eddie O'Sullivan guessing.

The Adelaide Oval, arguably the most attractive cricket ground in the world, hosted two contrasting rugby union games on successive days. Australia broke just about every record available as they trounced hapless Namibia 142-0. It was the biggest winning margin ever in a World Cup match, included the most ever tries scored with 22 and had tries from 11 different

RIGHT **Australian back Mat Rogers is tackled by Namibia's Melrick Africa with help from full back Ronaldo Pedro. Generally, though, the Africans were hopelessly outgunned, going down 142-0.**

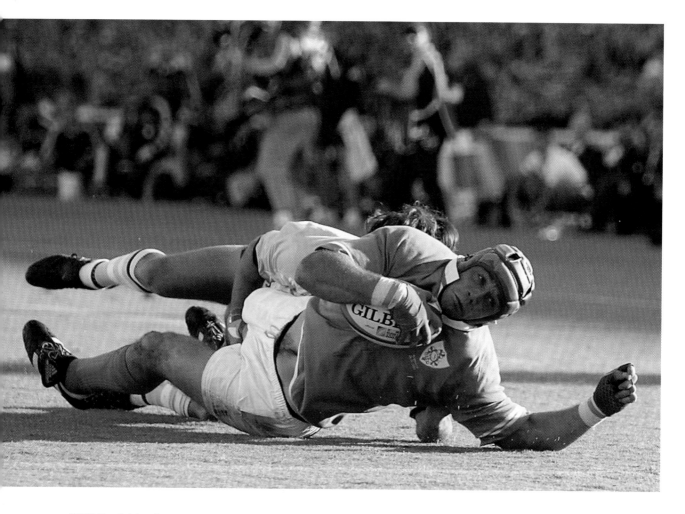

ABOVE **Alan Quinlan dives over to score his side's try in a tense encounter with Argentina that the Irish shaded 16-15. In scoring, though, the flanker dislocated his shoulder, ending his World Cup.**

players, also a record; but it was a scoreline that did very little for rugby in general. Namibia's coach, Dave Waterston, a self-confessed devotee of Johnnie Walker Black Label, decided, in typically cavalier fashion, to field his second-string outfit in order to keep his best team for the final game against Romania, but, while he continued to berate referees and administrators alike, everyone in Adelaide and beyond, including the most fervent of Australian supporters, was suitably embarrassed by the result.

Twenty-fours later, another capacity crowd witnessed an entirely different scenario, as Ireland and Argentina scrapped it out in the hardest-fought and most evenly contested game of the tournament to date. Simon Easterby and Alan Quinlan had done enough against Namibia to convince Eddie O'Sullivan that they should pack down in the back row on either side of Victor

Costello, who, in the continued absence of Anthony Foley, was preferred to Eric Miller at No. 8. Reggie Corrigan returned at loose-head and David Humphreys started once again, relegating Ronan O'Gara to the bench in the only change to the backs.

Argentina retained only right wing Jose Maria Nunez Piossek following the win against Romania four days earlier, but, ominously, they fielded nine of the side that had defeated Ireland in Lens in 1999 and had three more survivors from that game in the replacements panel. For the first time, the tension in the Irish camp was palpable, as an ashen-faced Keith Wood and his side struggled with the Pumas' power in the opening exchanges.

Ireland spilled a lot of ball, gave up possession too easily in the tackle, and were fortunate, thanks to superb discipline, to hold Argentina to a single penalty from Gonzalo Quesada in the opening quarter. Typically, it was Wood who brought Ireland their first score. After a scorching run from almost halfway and the sweetest of dummies, he sent Alan Quinlan in for a try which Humphreys goaled from the touch line. Alas, it was to be the highest and lowest point of Quinlan's World Cup, as the belligerent Munsterman dislocated his left shoulder in the process of touching down, ending his tournament there and then.

Eric Miller replaced Quinlan, and Humphreys stretched the Irish lead with a penalty, only for Quesada to squeeze over a dropped goal and land a penalty, leaving Ireland with an undeserved 10-9 lead at the interval. Further Argentinian pressure after the break allowed full back Ignacio Corleto the space to drop a goal to restore the lead for the Pumas, but with Ronan O'Gara taking over from David Humphreys, who had done little wrong, Ireland upped the pace and began to match their opponents in the forwards, with Paul O'Connell stealing valuable line-out ball.

O'Gara was having a bit of trouble with his line kicking, but he took the ball to the Pumas' midfield more effectively than Humphreys and kicked a couple of penalties for a 16-12 lead. Though Quesada landed a late penalty himself, the Pumas' challenge faded and the ghosts of Lens were well and truly exorcised. The pre-match tension was replaced with post-match relief in the knowledge that the Irish had reached the quarter-finals with a game in hand, while the Pumas, many of whom had played their last Test, had to pack their bags for home.

BELOW **Keith Wood, Ireland's talismanic skipper, rolls away from a maul against Argentina at the Adelaide Oval.**

ABOVE **Lucian Sirbu, Romania's scrum half, offloads during the match against Namibia. Sirbu scored in the Oaks' 37-7 win, which doomed the Africans to be Pool A's wooden spoonists.**
RIGHT **Wallaby lock Nathan Sharpe turns acrobat to snaffle line-out ball in the heart-stopping pool decider against Ireland at Melbourne's Telstra Dome.**

It wasn't quite over, since the Argentinian props Roberto Grau and Mauricio Reggiardo were cited for foul play – not, incidentally, by the Irish management – following a couple of nasty incidents involving Keith Wood and Reggie Corrigan. The term 'gouging' was never used, but video evidence seemed to indicate that Reggiardo had gone for Corrigan's eyes in a set scrummage and Grau had been similarly vicious towards Wood in loose play. Grau was subsequently suspended for nine weeks and Reggiardo for six, sentences which, given the accepted tariff for interfering with an opponent's eyes is twenty-four months, seemed extremely light.

Battered, bruised, exhausted, but above all, relieved, Ireland moved to Melbourne to prepare for their final pool game against the Wallabies. Eddie O'Sullivan's insistence that, with a quarter-final place assured, he wouldn't risk anyone who wasn't totally fit was interpreted as an indication that he would field an understrength side. But while Ireland had to discount the unfortunate Quinlan and Victor Costello, who had picked up a thigh injury, even Eddie Jones of Australia knew that O'Sullivan would be going all out for a win, with the prospect of an easier quarter-final against Scotland a huge incentive.

Anthony Foley returned at No. 8, having missed two games, Keith Gleeson replaced Quinlan, and O'Gara was in from the start, with Humphreys on the bench. Eddie Jones ignored media pressure and some fine individual performances against Namibia, particularly by Chris Latham, Stirling Mortlock and Lote Tuqiri, and went for the side that played Argentina, with Ben Darwin at tight-head prop the only change.

Some of the Irish squad went to the Melbourne Cricket Ground on the eve of their game with Australia to watch the Compromise Rules International between Ireland's Gaelic footballers and Australia's rugby league team; Ireland won the match but lost out on aggregate scores over two legs. The match was played in a downpour and the Irish ran out of steam in the final period, but the rugby squad knew that not only would they be capable of lasting 80 minutes against the Wallabies but the roof of the magnificent Telstra Dome would be closed the following evening, ensuring perfect conditions.

With 12 of the side that had beaten Australia in Dublin a year earlier, albeit in dreadful weather, Ireland had reason to be confident, but they looked, in the opening 15 minutes, like a side that was still recovering from the battle with Argentina. O'Gara, out of sorts with his touch-finding, missed an early penalty chance before the Wallabies went into a lead they were never to lose. Intense forward pressure gave George Gregan the chance to drop a goal, and within three minutes the Irish defence was sucked in, allowing George Smith an easy run-in at the corner.

O'Gara got Ireland on the scoreboard with a 16th-minute penalty, and while he and Flatley exchanged further penalties, O'Gara missed with a drop at goal and another penalty and Australia turned round 11-6 up. Wallaby full back Mat Rogers got himself sin-binned for killing the ball on the Irish side of a ruck. But instead of Ireland getting a very kickable penalty, touch judge Jonathan Kaplan intervened, and on his advice referee Paddy O'Brien sent Shane Horgan to the side line for ten minutes for careless footwork, and the penalty was reversed. Amidst all the furore, few noticed that Denis Hickie, whose clever running had taken Ireland close to the Wallaby line, was in trouble, and Ireland's record try scorer was helped off with a ruptured Achilles tendon. Both he and Alan Quinlan flew home two days later.

John Kelly, who replaced Hickie, was pressed into instant service as the Wallabies went on an early second-half offensive, with a Flatley penalty opening up an eight-point lead. However, it was Kelly's swift pass that gave a hitherto-shackled Brian O'Driscoll the room to squeeze over in the corner for his first try in ten games, with Wendell Sailor nowhere to be seen on the right wing. O'Gara converted splendidly, but Flatley's third penalty gave the Wallabies a bit of a cushion as they went 17-13 up.

'Waltzing O'Driscoll', as he was portrayed on giant Qantas posters around Australia, was playing more like the man who had wowed Australia with the Lions two years earlier and sneaked over a dropped goal to close the gap to a single point. The Irish, with O'Connell and Easterby pilfering at the Wallaby line out, gave it the proverbial 'lash' in the final ten minutes, and all of Australia

gasped as David Humphreys, who had replaced O'Gara, pushed a majestic dropped goal attempt just wide of the posts.

The final whistle from Paddy O'Brien, later criticised by Eddie O'Sullivan for a couple of penalties against Ireland in the final few minutes, couldn't come soon enough for Australia. Having won against Argentina when they perhaps didn't deserve to, Ireland could and should have beaten the Wallabies, who took the 17-16 win with both hands, leaving Eddie Jones to face a barrage of criticism for his forwards' failure to stay with Ireland in the final ten minutes and for the lack of penetration in his back division.

Eddie O'Sullivan, meanwhile, heaped praise on his troops for their overall efforts, reserving his wrath for those members of the written and electronic media who had damned Ireland with faint praise, using 'gallant' and 'plucky' to describe what came just short of being the upset of the tournament. Still, Ireland had eight days in which to prepare for their quarter-final against France. After what had happened four years earlier, it was no wonder that delirious Irish supporters drank the team hotel totally dry.

BELOW **'Waltzing O'Driscoll' beats Wallaby Elton Flatley's tackle to touch down early in the second half at Telstra Dome. The centre also dropped a goal as Ireland took the reigning champions all the way.**

Elton Flatley (AUS) – 18-second try v Romania.

What they said...

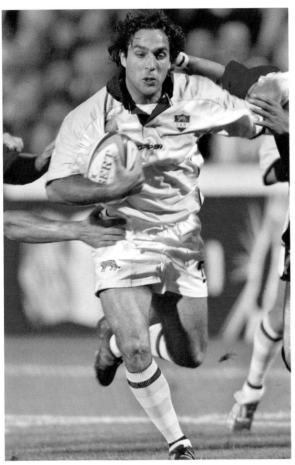

Martin Gaitan (ARG) – hat-trick v Namibia.

Australia: Eddie Jones (coach)

"We've had some easy contests and finished with a toughie against Ireland. But we keep winning and that's all that matters."

Ireland: Eddie O'Sullivan (coach)

"It is dismissive to describe us as plucky. Losing to Australia was only our third defeat in 21 Tests. We are not in the old days when we rushed around with our hair on fire. We can compete on the world stage."

Indignant Ireland coach Eddie O'Sullivan wants less patronising from the southern hemisphere.

Argentina: Marcelo Loffreda (coach)

"Australia dominated us in the tournament's opening game, meaning that we had to defeat Ireland. But in that key contest we failed to take our chances and lost by an agonising single point."

Romania: Romeo Gontineac (captain)

"Two years ago we had our darkest hour with the 134-0 defeat by England at Twickenham. We have improved noticeably since then."

Romania: Bernard Charreyre (coach)

"They deserved their win and this young group has everything in place to reach the last eight in 2007, even though the nation's player base is just 4,000."

Namibia: Sean Furter (captain)

"We had some depressing early defeats, and it was mentally hard to take. But we ended by giving Romania a game and earned some satisfaction."

Cricket score at the Adelaide Oval.

Les Bleus Rule the Roost

JILL DOUGLAS

ABOVE **The Scotland defence struggles in vain to prevent France fly half Frederic Michalak from crossing to register a full house of scores in his side's 51-9 victory in Sydney. Besides this try, Michalak's personal tally of 28 points for the game included four penalties, four conversions and a dropped goal.**

Scotland took extreme measures to ensure they were the best-prepared national squad ever to set out on a World Cup campaign. In the months leading up to their Australian adventure, the players experienced sub-zero temperatures in Poland and the tropical humidity of the hothouses in Edinburgh's Botanic Gardens.

Nothing would be left to chance as Ian McGeechan and Jim Telfer looked forward to their final fling on rugby's greatest stage. Both would step down after the tournament, Telfer into retirement and McGeechan away from coaching the national squad to become Scotland's director of rugby.

The World Cup would also signal the end of the international careers of some of Scotland's most loyal servants on the playing field. Captain and scrum half Bryan Redpath and wing Kenny Logan indicated this would be the rugby public's last chance to see them play for their country.

The Spala resort in Poland – already popular with Olympic athletes as well as other rugby and football teams – was where the hard work began. Players were eventually conditioned to spend up to three minutes at a time in the freezing-cold chambers, in which temperatures ended up a very long way below zero Celsius. These cryotherapy sessions are designed to dramatically shorten the players' recovery time after training, thereby enabling them to train harder and more often.

But the chill factor of Poland would not prepare the players for the high humidity and soaring temperatures predicted for Townsville, the venue for their opening match against Japan. To cope with those conditions, the players acclimatised in the hothouses of Edinburgh's Royal Botanic Garden. It was an added attraction for the visitors to these famous gardens to see 30 rugby players on treadmills and rowing machines among the tropical foliage. So full marks to fitness coach Marty Hulme for preparing the squad for Australia, but as for the matches leading up to the tournament – well, the report card read 'Must do better'.

A mediocre Six Nations campaign, with defeats against France, England and Ireland, was followed by a promising summer tour to South Africa. Two solid performances against the Springboks breathed fresh optimism into the Scotland camp and saw the emergence of new talent – and a new lease of life for some of the most experienced players in the side.

Scotland outscored South Africa by three tries to two at the ABSA Stadium in Durban, only to lose narrowly by 29 points to 25. A week later, and they again pushed the Springboks all the way at Ellis Park, losing by 28 points to 19. Special mention was made of the way Glenn Metcalfe, Chris Paterson and Kenny Logan combined at the back, while Bruce Douglas and Gavin Kerr showed great promise. At the time, Ian McGeechan commented, 'We have progressed but there can be no complacency in any mistaken belief that we have cracked it.'

The most disappointing element of the tour was the injury to captain Bryan Redpath in the Johannesburg Test match. A torn bicep ruled him out of Scotland's World Cup warm-up matches. And the scrum half was missed by his team-mates in the three build-up games. Edinburgh's Mike Blair undoubtedly has a bright future ahead of him behind the scrum, but Redpath is a world-class scrum half and commands the respect of his team and opponents alike.

Blair, however, was in excellent form against Italy as Scotland ran in six tries at Murrayfield. Bath's flying winger Simon Danielli, with a try-scoring debut, emerged as a strong and positive runner. But against Wales and Ireland the Scots took several steps backwards, and set out for Australia on the back of two disappointing defeats.

RIGHT **Flashpoint at Suncorp. France flanker Olivier Magne reels backwards as Fiji's Rupeni Caucaunibuca lashes out. In the short term both players were despatched to the sin-bin, but Caucau was later banned for two matches.**

At first glance the Scots should have been reasonably content with their draw, finding themselves alongside France, Japan, Fiji and the USA in Pool B. For the fourth time in five tournaments they had avoided one of the heavyweights of the southern hemisphere in the group stage. France were heavily fancied to win the pool, though in the event of Scotland finishing on top, the latter could anticipate a quarter-final in Melbourne against the runners-up in Pool A, which included the superpowers of Australia, Argentina and Ireland. If Scotland secured second place in their pool, then it would be a quarter-final meeting in Brisbane with the winners of Pool A. D-Day was likely to be 28 October and their match with France in Sydney.

ABOVE **Urged on by Christophe Dominici, who himself scored twice in the game, Yannick Jauzion runs in one of his three tries in France's 61-18 defeat of Fiji. The centre's hat-trick came in a 16-minute period in the second half.**

The Scots arrived in Queensland ahead of their opening match against Japan and set up camp in Coloundra. But instead of the warm sunshine they had expected, they encountered cool and breezy conditions – and they received a sharp wake-up call about what to expect later in their pool when France and Fiji met in Brisbane's Suncorp Stadium to get their group under way.

Always a handful, this Fijian side included the powerful figure of Rupeni Caucaunibuca, who was expected to make quite a name for himself at this World Cup. Unfortunately the winger grabbed the headlines for all the wrong reasons. After a moment of brilliance, charging 75 yards to score one of the best tries of

the tournament, came a moment of madness. The Fijian landed two blows on French flanker Olivier Magne, who hit back. The result: Magne was floored and the two ended up in the sin-bin. The incident earned Caucau a three-match ban, though this was eventually shortened to two matches, ominously allowing him to return to the Fijian line-up for the match against the Scots in Sydney on 1 November. Meanwhile, at Suncorp, France were comfortable winners 61-18, running in seven tries, setting out their ambitions for this World Cup and showing that in Magne, Betsen and Harinordoquy they could field arguably the best back row in the competition.

Little was known of the strength of the Japanese. Smaller in stature and still developing as a rugby nation, they were coached by Shogo Mukai. But the presence of Wallaby legend Mark Ella in Japan's coaching team should have sounded a few warning bells. The Cherry Blossoms were not here just to make up the numbers.

The Dairy Farmers Stadium in Townsville was the venue for Scotland's opening fling against the Japanese side, playing in their fifth World Cup and looking to secure only their second victory to add to their win over Zimbabwe in 1991. It was a far from comfortable start for the Scots and served as a warning to their fans that they would need nerves of steel to follow their progress in Australia. The 20,000 crowd were firmly behind the Cherry Blossoms, and Japan's endeavours were best illustrated by Hirotoki Onozawa's classic back-line try following some unrelenting defence from his team-mates. It brought the score to

BELOW **Api Naevo thanks heaven after scoring Fiji's try against the USA. The islanders shaded the match 19-18 after a grandstand finish by the Eagles brought a last-gasp try that they could not convert.**

15-11 and thrilled the partisan crowd. But the Scots battled on, and Chris Paterson's opportunist try 14 minutes from time steadied the ship. Simon Taylor scored on 75 minutes to give Scotland a more respectable margin of 32-11.

Players will look back at moments of this competition and ponder what might have been; none more so than USA fly half Mike Hercus. His last-minute conversion attempt against Fiji in Brisbane sailed wide as the Eagles narrowly lost 19-18 to the South Sea islanders. Had it been on target, it would have brought about the USA's first RWC win since they beat Japan in 1987. Alas it was not to be and Fiji scraped through, coach Mac McCallion admitting, 'I've aged ten years on the night.'

There was a more comfortable margin of victory for France in a hot and humid Townsville when they took on Japan. Many had predicted a cricket score, but the Cherry Blossoms again showed their resolve, and France were made to sweat with their lead no more than 20-19 early in the second half. However, Japan tired as the match drew to a close and France eventually ran in six tries –

Aurelien Rougerie with two – to win 51-29. But the best score of the night belonged to Japan's flying wing, Daisuke Ohata.

Scotland, meanwhile, were dealing with two fresh problems. Flanker Andrew Mower suffered a serious knee injury in training and was ruled out of the whole competition, requiring surgery before flying home. His replacement, Glasgow captain Cameron Mather, arrived on the morning of the Scots' second match, against the USA. The Scots were also forced to move hotels earlier than planned when they were warned that a bikers' gathering at their Coloundra base could prove disruptive. 'Fainthearts' was the headline back in Scotland.

RIGHT **No way out. Scotland fly half Gregor Townsend is comprehensively wrapped up by the USA defence this time but provided some moments of magic in his side's 39-15 victory.**
BELOW **France did not have it all their own way against Japan, who scored two tries against Les Bleus, including a cracker by Daisuke Ohata (centre), seen here in a foot race with Christophe Dominici.**

But it was an improved performance against the Eagles, though ultimately the game proved costly indeed as the Scots lost another of their back-rowers – and this time there was no replacement allowed. Martin Leslie was cited after the match for illegal use of the knee on American centre Jason Keyter. A twelve-week ban, later reduced to eight, brought to an end the international career of this popular and much-admired rugby player. It also raised many questions about the citing process and sparked debate on whether there was an even hand at play in the dispensing of punishments, following Caucau's two-match ban for the earlier incident. 'Martin was retiring from the international game at the end of the World Cup and it saddens me that it appears he may have to bow out under such circumstances. As a group we feel hard done by,' said McGeechan.

On a brighter note, the game against the USA allowed Bath's Simon Danielli to show his considerable skills and promise on the international stage. The 6ft 4ins wing struck twice in the first half to take his try count for Scotland to four in four games as Scotland ran out 39-15 winners. The game also saw Gregor Townsend back to near his best and put him firmly ahead of Gordon Ross for the stand-off berth, while Ross's Leeds team-mate Gavin Kerr scored his first international try. Kerr was fortunate that his captain, Bryan Redpath, wasn't too close by when he touched down under the posts. Redpath – or 'Basil', as he is known – can be a cheeky fellow and earned himself the new nickname of 'The Nutcracker' after giving Chris Paterson an intimate squeeze when he scored his try. The penalty count against the Scots was again too high and they conceded afterwards that it would take a much more disciplined performance to cause France any serious problems in Sydney.

Following the defeat by France, the Cherry Blossoms' coach, Shogo Mukai, made seven changes to his starting line-up for the match against Fiji. But the Fijians were too strong, outscoring Japan by five tries to one to win 41-13. As the Japanese departed their Townsville camp, they left many new friends behind. One local schoolboy in particular will never forget their contribution to RWC 2003. He made a grand entrance to the Townsville High School formal, ex-sumo wrestler and now Japanese prop Ryo Yamamura delivering him there in a shopping trolley.

Scotland's date with France at Telstra Stadium in Sydney was always going to be the key to this pool, and as the French prepared for the showdown at their base in Bondi, the Scots were

RIGHT **France's Olivier Magne carves through the Scottish defence and heads for the line with fellow back-rowers Imanol Harinordoquy and Serge Betsen (the eventual try scorer) in support.**

ABOVE **USA hooker Kirk Khasigian, whose father, Fred, was also an Eagle, hands off a Japanese defender as the Americans power to their first World Cup win since 1987 (when they also beat Japan).**

in sleepy Cronulla. With Mower back in Scotland and Leslie out of the competition, Ian McGeechan had some tough decisions to make in his back-row selection, especially as Jon Petrie was struggling with a shoulder injury. So Cameron Mather, barely over his jet lag, found himself at open-side flanker for one of Scotland's biggest ever World Cup games – and facing the world-class trio of Betsen, Magne and Harinordoquy. But there was no start for Danielli, Kenny Logan being preferred on the wing.

The day itself was like a fairly typical Edinburgh spring day – a cold start with torrential rain failing to dampen the spirits of the thousands of Scotland fans at the stadium. However, it was not their day as a classy French outfit swept the Scots aside and gave a timely warning to the rest of the world to sit up and take note. Before kick-off the Scots paid tribute to banned flanker Martin Leslie, by copying his trademark facial twitch as the television cameras swept along the Scottish line during the anthems. It was a mark of respect to a great servant to Scottish rugby and a reminder of the team spirit that binds these players together. They would need all their resolve in the 80 minutes to follow.

The Scots started well and defended bravely and were trailing only 3-0 after a dropped goal from fly half Frederic Michalak on 15 minutes. But inevitably Les Bleus cut loose, and it was that deadly trio of French back-rowers who combined to score their opening try – Magne surging through the midfield, offloading to Imanol Harinordoquy, who fed Serge Betsen, who charged over to score. Breathtaking. A Paterson penalty kept the Scots in the hunt, but Michalak replied to send the French into the break with a 19-6 lead.

A Nicolas Brusque dropped goal extended that to 22-6 as the French stepped up a gear and began to pile on the pressure. This resulted in a try for Harinordoquy from a rolling maul to the Scottish line. Michalak recorded a full house of scores with a try himself under the posts, and Fabien Galthie danced over unopposed from a five-metre scrum to add to the Scots' agony. The half-century was reached when Brusque went over in the corner and Michalak rounded off a fine personal performance with the conversion. The Scots never looked like crossing the French try line and had only three Paterson penalties to show for their efforts in a 51-9 defeat. It left France sitting comfortably on top of the group and gave the Scots a week to prepare for the winner-takes-all match with Fiji to decide who would go through to the quarters-finals with France.

Japan's final fling at RWC 2003 came against the USA in the beautifully situated Central Coast Stadium in Gosford. The contribution made by the Japanese to this competition was reflected in the support shown by the Australian fans who donned white and red bandanas for the game. Mark Ella said, 'I think a lot of Australians liked the fact that they never gave up and were so determined. But they do need to bulk up a bit.' That was never more evident than in the last quarter of their match with the USA when the giant Eagles winger Riaan van Zyl repeatedly charged down the touch line to be denied by terrific cover tackles from the much smaller and much lighter Japanese winger Toru Kurihara. Finally, though, van Zyl proved too strong and scored with four minutes to go, the Eagles recording their first win of the tournament in their final game by 39 points to 26. No win for the Japanese, but they surprised a few and will be back better and perhaps bigger in 2007.

France looked less convincing in their final pool match against the USA at Wollongong but maintained their 100 per cent record as Brian Liebenberg ran in a hat-trick of tries. It was the centre's first start and he made a strong statement of intent to coach Bernard Laporte, who had fielded very much a second-string side for the match. The Eagles twice breached the French defence and never capitulated. However, Les Bleus were too strong and earned an unimpressive 41-14 victory to top Pool B.

The losers of Scotland v Fiji would need to go through qualification to reach RWC 2007, so much was at stake in this match and it went all the way down to the wire. In the end, though, the superior fitness, discipline and experience of the

BELOW **Rupeni Caucaunibuca kicks ahead behind Scotland's Glenn Metcalfe at Aussie Stadium, Sydney. His ban completed, the Fijian returned with two tries but was unable to prevent a Scottish win.**

Scots made the difference, and even though it took 78 minutes to secure the victory, the phrase 'Never in doubt' rang around the stadium afterwards among relieved and emotionally drained Scottish fans.

McGeechan decided to accommodate Danielli and Logan and moved Chris Paterson to stand-off for the clash, with Townsend at outside centre. This would, he hoped, ignite the Scots' back line. But Fiji started magnificently and could easily have had the match out of Scotland's reach in an explosive first 20 minutes. After serving his two-match suspension, Rupeni Caucaunibuca was back in action and desperate to atone for his earlier disgrace. He scored his side's two tries, the first coming from a forward pass but the second from a devastating 50-metre run before half-time. Nicky Little converted both, while Chris Paterson's penalties kept Scotland in the match. Any chances Scotland managed to engineer they also managed to spoil, and Fiji found themselves 20-15 up as the game headed to a thrilling finale. Fijian indiscipline finally resulted in the sin-binning of Api Naevo, and with a one-man advantage Scotland piled on the pressure, Tom Smith eventually barging over with his pack's support with only two minutes left on the clock. Scotland's points difference would have seen them through in the event of a draw, but Chris Paterson finished off a fine all-round performance with an accurate conversion to make the final score 22-20. Afterwards captain Bryan Redpath conceded, 'It was very close. It shows you have to dig deep in games like this, but credit to Fiji – they got two opportunities in the first half and that man Caucau just killed us.' So Scotland through to face Australia in Brisbane. Never in doubt.

BELOW **With two minutes to go to full-time, Scotland cross the Fijian line in the shape of Tom Smith (hidden from view) and book their place in the quarter-finals.**

Brian Liebenberg (FRA) – hat-trick v USA.

What they said...

Scotland: Dougie Morgan (manager)

"It has been a very happy World Cup for us and we are even happier to have safely qualified."

The Scotland manager rubbishes reports of disharmony between players and management.

France: Bernard Laporte (coach)

"I do not have a B team or an A team. My squad are all worthy Test players."

The France coach stresses a point after stories of discontent among players being regularly omitted.

Kort Schubert (USA) – last-minute try v Fiji.

USA: Dave Hodges (captain)

"We accomplished at least one of our goals with the success against Japan after falling that single point short against the very good Fijians. Then we hit the wall against a real class act in France."

Japan: Mark Ella (coach)

"It's so frustrating always to let the opposition create a lead in the first quarter, by which time the game's gone. It's going to take a lot of hard work and more games against the top nations for us to improve our status."

Fiji: Greg Smith (hooker)

"We had it in our power to qualify, but we let it slip against Scotland. It was a big day and the world was watching. We didn't come through and the disappointment is immense."

Takeomi Ito (JPN) v Scott Murray (SCO).

47

Some things get better given longer.

Brewed longer
for a distinctive,
full flavour

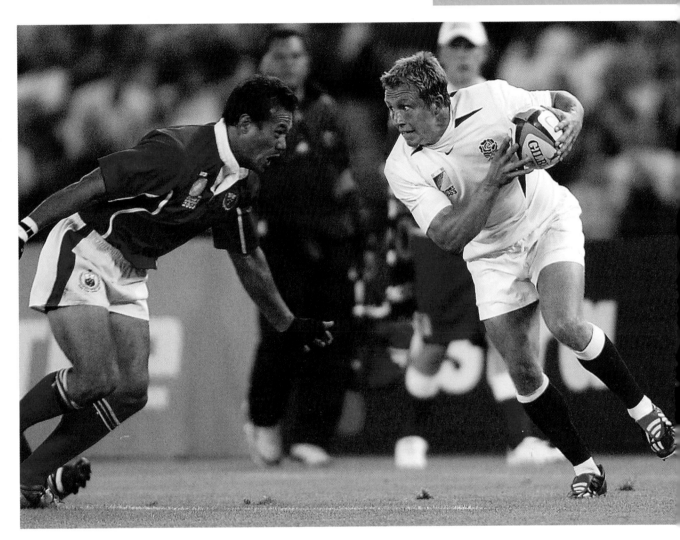

ABOVE **Jonny Wilkinson under pressure as England reap the Samoan whirlwind at Telstra Dome, Melbourne. The men in white emerged safely on the other side but not without a struggle.**

I n the mind's eye it was quite simple. Big-browed, four-square South Africans, bristling with a sense of grievance and history, were all that stood between England and a romp into the Rugby World Cup quarter-finals. These men would come together in a sense of righteous indignation at being cast as outsiders and prove to the world once again what a force South African rugby actually was. In their sights was the pampered, colonial, bumptious enemy – England. Clive Woodward's men in white had beaten the Boks four times in succession, the last of these victories being a spiteful affair at Twickenham. South Africa had had a man sent off – lock Jannes Labuschagne. The fall-out

was fractious as the South Africans stood in the dock accused of all sorts of vicious misdemeanours. The rematch had a lot riding on it. Yes, this would be the game of Pool C, the only thing that mattered, as these two rivals squared up.

And then along came Samoa. Thank goodness for the Pacific islanders. Pool C needed them, as did Rugby World Cup 2003. The Georgians and Uruguayans played their part too in what was

ABOVE **The face of determination. Ben Cohen takes on Springbok centre Jorrie Muller as England impose themselves on South Africa at the Subiaco Oval, Perth.**

an intriguing group. But it was Samoa that gave the pool real credibility and edge. It was not that England's game against South Africa did not live up to expectations. It hit the mark on all counts – a hard, bruising encounter won by England 25-6. But for all the tension and close-quarter defiance of the Springboks, the outcome was as we might have expected. England prevailed through their greater sense of composure and togetherness. When the game came to crunch time around the hour mark, it was England who were able to find something else; it was England who knew how to turn the screw one notch more.

As for Samoa, they didn't give a damn about pre-match theory. They didn't give a monkey's about pre-match reputation. They didn't care that, man for man, they had neither the pedigree, the conditioning nor the wage packet of their illustrious opponents. They had each other and they had their belief. Samoa reminded us that this game is about heart and soul as much as it

is about resources and money. They reminded us too that it is possible to play this game with a smile on the face, even if there is thunder in every tackle.

Let us dwell on what happened that Sunday night at Telstra Dome in Melbourne. For it was a game – won by England, 35-22 – that will be remembered for many a day. It had a significance, too, way beyond the confines of the pool. It made us realise that the game needs the Samoas of the world. In this pool we also saw enough good things from Georgia and Uruguay to realise that rugby has a presence and a reality beyond its traditional empire. Those outposts too must not be allowed to shrivel.

But if the rugby world ever allows Samoa to disappear off the map, then it should hang its head in shame. Just when this Rugby World Cup was in danger of subsiding into an embarrassing catalogue of pantomime matches along come Samoa, and with them, true drama. There was a tense narrative, complex character development and an outcome that was in doubt until the closing stages. England, who trailed 16-13 at the interval, only really wrapped the game up with replacement prop Phil Vickery's try six minutes from time.

The upshot was that England's lofty ambitions to lift the Webb Ellis trophy diminished in the eyes of several witnesses, notably the watching Australian and New Zealand camps, both of whom were in town. Mind you, captain Martin Johnson was none too impressed either. 'That was not good enough,' said Johnson. 'Full credit to Samoa. They could have beaten us. We're not going to win anything if we play like that.'

Johnson has never traded in flimflam. He didn't on the night either, producing one of the few England performances of note. Jonny Wilkinson proved a barometer of English fortunes. He rarely hit any meaningful rhythm, albeit he was scrabbling for decent possession for long stretches of the first half. But if that was worrying enough for the many thousands of England fans in the crowd of 50,647, then it was the sight of Mr Dead-Eye having an attack of the wobbles right in front of the posts that really set them on edge. Wilkinson missed one kick from point-blank range and only marginally off-centre, the ball striking the left upright. The resulting thud found a hollow echo in the pit of many England stomachs. In all, four kicks failed to find their target.

Samoa never let England settle. The men in white were discordant through the midfield and flustered in their control of the ball. Their penalty count was once again far higher than their usual single-figure target. England were lucky not to be yellow-carded. The ledger of negatives was substantial.

Samoa rattled England not just in the tackle but also at the breakdown. The English back row was not operating at full tilt.

BELOW **Turning point. England flanker Lewis Moody hurls himself at Springbok fly half Louis Koen's kick, charging it down to create the game's only try for Will Greenwood.**

ABOVE **The moment that stunned the rugby world. Skipper Semo Sititi breaches England's much-vaunted defence to score for Samoa.** FACING PAGE **Phil Vickery crosses for his first international score to give England breathing space at last against the battling Samoans.**

Lawrence Dallaglio knew only too well that he was not reaching the standards he set on the summer tour.

Samoa could consider themselves hard done by in the award of a penalty try against them for collapsing a scrum in the 52nd minute. They had had no warning from referee Jonathan Kaplan, who otherwise had a fine evening. 'That try was a turning point,' said Samoa captain Semo Sititi. Earlier Sititi had scored one of the tries of this or any other World Cup. His touchdown in the sixth minute came at the end of an 11-phase sequence, the ball passing through 40 pairs of Samoan hands.

Samoa put together a mean game of rugby as well as bringing their normal sense of exuberance to the party. Sititi's back-row mates, Maurie Fa'asavalu and Peter Poulos, were prominent all over the field. Half backs Steven So'oialo and Earl Va'a were sharp and authoritative in all that they did. Centre Brian Lima, in his record 15th successive World Cup game, never missed a beat.

And all this from a scratch side. This was not a Samoan team of stars as it was in the early 1990s. They are an ad hoc combination, drawn from the four corners, who play with one heart. Coach John Boe did a magnificent job. The cruellest cut of the night was that Samoa didn't gain a bonus point.

Samoa were ten points to the good within six minutes. Va'a's early penalty was followed by Sititi's try. It was a rich prelude, the move beginning within the Samoa 22 and zigzagging across field with splendid assistance notably from full back Tanner Vili, wing Lome Fa'atau and prop Kas Lealamanu'a.

England had to grind their way into contention, and did so in faithful style, Neil Back touching down at the end of a line-out maul in the 25th minute. An exchange of penalty goals saw Samoa keep their noses in front.

The penalty try sapped the first drops of Samoan morale, even though Va'a did manage to knock over two penalties in quick succession midway through the second half. Wilkinson's smart dropped goal in the 64th minute triggered a sequence of uninterrupted England scoring. Iain Balshaw latched on to a pinpoint Wilkinson cross-field kick to run in unmolested. The arrival of Mike Catt on the field brought some width to movements, with the Bath centre involved three times in the build-up to Vickery's first ever try for England. It was 35-22 at the final whistle, and the relief was plain to see on England faces.

The post-match reaction told its own tale. 'Samoa asked us questions that we have not been asked for a long, long time,' said England captain Martin Johnson. 'We had to dig ourselves out of

RIGHT **Samoa's coach, former Waikato stand-off John Boe, is concerned for the future of the island's rugby: 'I'm very fearful that Samoa will not be able to field a side at the next World Cup in 2007.'** BELOW **Dan Luger stands by to come on against Samoa. His introduction while Mike Tindall was still receiving onfield treatment led to England having 16 players on the pitch and the subsequent imposition of a £10,000 fine by Rugby World Cup Ltd.**

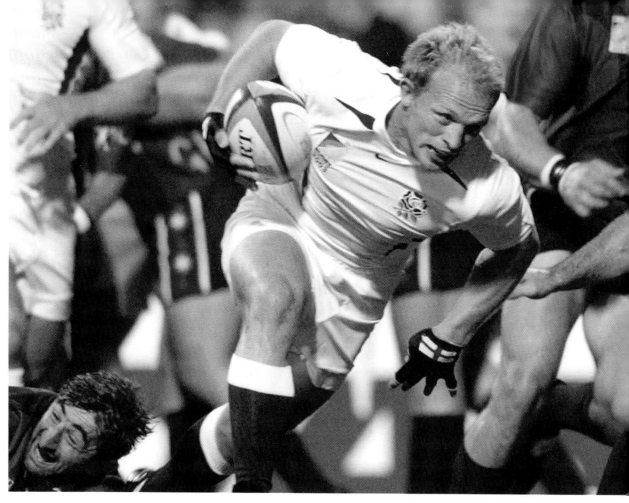

a hole. We were 10-0 down and hadn't touched the ball. It's a hard game to play without the ball. It's been a long time since I can remember playing against a team that did so well in the first 20 minutes. Samoa have the ability to go the length of the field and that's what happened. We made too many mistakes and need to look at ourselves as players.'

Clive Woodward had taken nothing for granted. 'The only people who gave Samoa due credit beforehand were ourselves with our strong selection,' said the England head coach. 'We know we've got a lot to improve.'

Samoa were as they had been all week – dignified and honest. 'We'd like to think that we made a statement tonight and that statement is that our team deserves to survive,' said coach John Boe.

There was nobody in the entire land who would dispute that. Boe was a wonderful ambassador for Samoan rugby throughout the entire tournament. He spent the week of the England build-up articulating all the vivid concerns of the island people. If there is any legacy from Rugby World Cup 2003, the words of Boe should be a central part of it.

'I'm very fearful that Samoa will not be able to field a side at the next World Cup in 2007,' says Boe, a 47-year-old former Waikato fly half who was seconded by the New Zealand Rugby

Union in 2000 to help with the development of Samoan rugby. He was so outspoken about the self-interested attitudes of New Zealand that his contract at home has not been renewed.

'The problem of player availability is becoming more and more acute. There are guys playing provincial rugby in New Zealand that we just can't get our hands on. There is no doubt that the New Zealand union see us a feeder. We have no issue whatsoever about a Samoan boy who becomes an All Black. That is a wonderful thing for them, and for the honour of Samoa. It is all the other players that get wrapped up. The International Rugby Board can't just walk away from this. They have to do something, and do something soon.'

Boe would like to see several of the eligibility issues revisited so that a player might play again for Samoa after, perhaps, a three year stand-down period since representing New Zealand or whoever. That would mean that the likes of Andrew Blowers, the Northampton flanker, could turn out for Samoa.

LEFT **Matt Dawson about to score against Georgia. A leg injury picked up in the match kept him out of the clash with South Africa.** BELOW **The South Africa and Georgia packs about to collide at Aussie Stadium. The Boks won this match, unconvincingly, 46-19.**

2003

'There is a bloodline there that might be lost to rugby and it would be a tragedy,' says Boe. 'These guys are born to play rugby. They develop physically earlier than Europeans and enjoy the smash element of the game. They have a natural instinct for the ball and are athletic on the move. Do we want to lose all that? Remember, too, that rugby is not just a game in Samoa. It is a central part of their culture. It is the one thing that they have contributed to the world.'

The Samoans are cherished wherever they go – for the vigour of their play and the warmth of their spirit. 'They have taught me so much about humility and respect,' says Boe. 'I don't envy what England or New Zealand might have in terms of resources. Our boys never, ever complain. And their passion for the game, their commitment to each other and to their country, is truly uplifting.'

PREVIOUS PAGES **Joy is unconfined as Uruguay record their second World Cup win (they beat Spain in 1999), defeating Georgia 24-12.** BELOW **Alfonso Cardoso outflanks Paliko Jimsheladze to score the first of Uruguay's three tries against Georgia.**

Samoa had too much class and pace in their other pool games, beating Uruguay 60-13 and Georgia 46-9.

The two other teams in Pool C emerged with credit. Georgia – intelligently led by No. 8 Ilia Zedginidze – were a tough forward outfit who made sure that England had plenty of bruises the morning after their 84-6 victory. The scoreboard didn't tell the full story of that testing encounter.

The Georgians were unable to sustain their full-bore game throughout the pool stages, despite putting up a magnificent show against South Africa before going down 46-19. However, they were almost a spent force by the time they came up against Uruguay four days later, the South Americans winning 24-12 and scoring three tries in the process. Georgia would have hoped for more, but the experience of the Uruguayans in their second appearance at a World Cup saw them home.

Uruguay, well led by centre Diego Aguirre and with No. 8 Rodrigo Capo an influential presence, had targeted that game. They had subsided tamely to Samoa, 60-13, and were desperate not to draw a blank. 'That was our final,' said Aguirre.

Earl Va'a (SAM) – 17 points v England.

What they said...

England: Clive Woodward (coach)

"The phoney war is over. We have achieved our objective of playing our quarter-final in Brisbane. South Africa was obviously the key match and it was satisfying to keep them tryless in an excellent defensive effort in the pool game."

South Africa: Joost van der Westhuizen (scrum half)

"I've played alongside some of the great Springboks kickers and this young man could be up there with the best."
On new kicker Derick Hougaard, who scored a 'full house' against Samoa.

Brian 'The Chiropractor' Lima (SAM) at work v Georgia.

Samoa: John Boe (coach)

"After taking England all the way we had a reality check against South Africa, when we let our fans down. We need finance, more Tests and to retain more players."

Uruguay: Diego Aguirre (captain)

"It was logical to focus all our efforts on Georgia and we emerged with an encouraging win."

Uruguay: Diego Ormaechea (coach)

"Against England it was Formula One against a bicycle – a lion against a mouse. We are a soccer nation with only 300 rugby players."

Georgia: Ilia Zedginidze (captain)

"Playing in the World Cup was an excellent experience. The team grew up and match by match we did better, though without getting a win."

Josh Lewsey (ENG) – five tries v Uruguay.

STEPHEN JONES

ABOVE **Hands up who scored. A delighted Kees Meeuws crosses for one of New Zealand's ten tries in the 68-6 victory over Canada at Telstra Dome in Melbourne.**

It appeared at one stage that Pool D action would peter out at the end. The final match in the group was between New Zealand and Wales. Not only had Wales failed to beat New Zealand since 1953, but most of the subsequent matches between the two countries had ended in resounding thrashings for Wales; and when the two teams ran out onto the field at a sold-out Telstra Stadium in Sydney, many pundits were predicting at least a 50-point margin for the All Blacks, sending them safely through to the quarter-finals after a dominating performance in their pool matches.

The reality was different, and also extraordinary. It had always been a thrilling World Cup and a thrilling pool, but the New Zealand-Wales game on its own lifted the whole tournament to new heights. For the record, New Zealand won 53-37 after an absolutely brilliant match in which many of the Welsh team played far above any known form. But if the final score looks relatively comfortable (for all bar the defensive coaches on each side), then it must be remembered that Wales were leading 37-33 inside the final quarter and seemed to be opening up the New Zealand defence with some ease.

Indeed, it was only with a highly controversial score that New Zealand were able to re-establish themselves, having regained the lead by a single point through a Carlos Spencer try in the 61st minute. Justin Marshall made a break towards the Welsh left-hand corner and it seemed for all the world that the pass with which he slipped Doug Howlett over in the corner was forward – certainly, television commentators, spectators level with the action and all replays indicated that the pass was comfortably illegal. However, play continued, and another late All Black try gave the final scoreline a considerably flattering appearance from the New Zealand point of view.

There were eight New Zealand tries to four by Wales, but the Welsh spirit was indomitable, and after some early lapses the Welsh defence battled brilliantly against what had been, in the tournament so far, a Kiwi attacking machine. Players like Rob Sidoli and Mark Taylor were in world-class form for Wales, but two of the most remarkable performances came from players on the fringes of the squad.

Jonathan Thomas, the young Neath/Swansea Ospreys flanker, had a staggering match, often breaking through deep New Zealand cover with charges of remarkable power. On the wing, the diminutive Shane Williams was possibly even better. Williams made many slashing runs, bewildering the New Zealand defence with his flair and confidence.

The post-match inquest posed the fascinating question as to whether this brilliant Welsh revival performance had been orchestrated by Steve Hansen, the beleaguered Welsh coach, or had been the fruits of a Welsh team deciding almost subliminally to play things off the cuff. Whatever the answer, everyone in the Welsh camp deserved the utmost credit. At the end, New Zealand were safely through, as leaders of Pool D, into their quarter-final match against South Africa. However, they were badly shaken, and it seemed that the weaknesses illuminated in their team might just prove costly as the knockout stages approached.

The Welsh try scorers were Mark Taylor, Sonny Parker, Colin Charvis and Shane Williams himself, although they could easily have scored two or three more. Wales's ball retention and patience in the face of a highly rated New Zealand defence were remarkable, and, frankly, it was difficult to believe that this was the same Welsh team that had often struggled against lesser opposition in the pool.

But New Zealand deserved credit for pulling themselves together. In many ways, this was the match that they needed, coming at the very end of the pool action. They had been unchallenged in the group to date, in large part because Canada,

RIGHT **Flying All Black wing Joe Rokocoko prepares for landing to open New Zealand's try count against Wales. With his second score of the game he passed the All Black record for tries in a calendar year – 12 by Christian Cullen and Jonah Lomu.**

2003

Tonga and Italy had all fielded weakened sides against them. This was done on the unsatisfactory but also realistic and understandable premise that if teams had no chance of beating New Zealand anyway, then why would they throw in their very best players to risk injury, when the key matches for those lesser teams would come when they played each other?

Of the eight New Zealand tries, Joe Rokocoko and Doug Howlett scored two each, illustrating the power down the All Blacks' flanks. The remainder came from Leon MacDonald, Ali Williams, Carlos Spencer and Aaron Mauger, the last-mentioned making a welcome first appearance in the tournament after an injury sustained in training before the action began.

But the ebb and flow of this titanic tussle, the sheer courage and endeavour and technical excellence, left an indelible impression. Whatever was to happen later in the tournament, it was the match that gave New Zealand a thorough shakedown, and it was the match that gave Welsh rugby just a hint of better things around the corner. Frankly, before the World Cup it was difficult to see how Wales would ever again manage to live with New Zealand.

Here, they lived with them for around 70 of the 80 minutes of action. It was quite wonderful stuff. Wales had their good fortune earlier in the pool. It emerged that they and Italy were the prime contenders for second place in the group and, therefore, for qualification for the quarter-finals and a match, as it turned out, against England in Brisbane. Most observers judged that Italy were more impressive than Wales in the early pool action. However, actual technical excellence was to count as nothing. Italy were well and truly scuppered by what was for them a wounding and even scandalous fixture list in which they were forced to play four matches inside fourteen days.

It was an itinerary that none of the major rugby nations would ever have agreed to, but Italy's complaints months before the tournament fell on stern and deaf ears. Syd Millar, chairman of Rugby World Cup, was honest enough to admit after Italy's premature ejection from the tournament that the fixture list had been bitterly unfair to them. Millar pointed out that the major rugby-playing nations brought in the bulk of TV revenue and that teams like Wales and England and the other foundation rugby nations were required to play at peak times, and especially on the weekend, to placate the god of television.

Italy's big game was always to be their encounter with Wales in Canberra, but this match came a mere four days after the Azzurri had battled to a 19-14 victory over Canada. Crucially, Wales had a full 48 hours more than Italy to prepare for their vital

FACING PAGE **Robert Sidoli provides for Wales. Both he and centre Mark Taylor were in great form against the All Blacks.**
BELOW **New Zealand wing Doug Howlett crosses for one of his brace in the 53-37 thriller against Colin Charvis's men.**

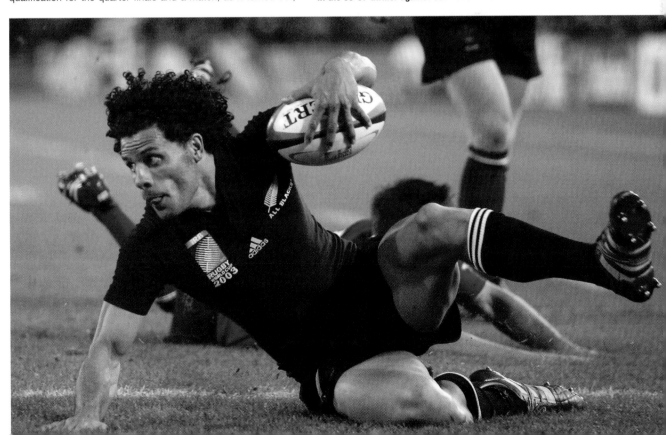

ABOVE **A dejected-looking Santiago Dellape, the Italian lock, sits on the replacement's bench, having been substituted, as his side go down against Wales in Canberra.**

game. Those 48 hours were all priceless. Generally speaking, the days of international teams playing twice or even three times inside a fortnight are long gone, and to order a side to play four times inside a fortnight is only to crucify that team.

The result of the crunch match in the play-off for second place was 27-15 to Wales. Italy began brightly, and with a little more steadiness, could easily have scored three tries inside the opening 20 minutes. There was a solidity about their scrummage and an enterprise about their backs, among whom Denis Dallan was influential. Yet it all came to nothing because after their initial jousts Italy were palpably lacking in spring in the step and long before the end of the match were clearly exhausted and going through the motions.

Wales scored three tries, through Dafydd Jones, Sonny Parker and Mark Jones, while Italy had to be content with

15 points all from kicks. In fact Italy had revealed a fine crop of new players during the tournament, but Wales were able almost to coast home in Canberra and take their place in the quarter-finals. We will never know if Italy would have proceeded had they been playing on a level field, but John Kirwan, a wise bird, clearly spotted the problems months before the tournament, and all his gloomiest predictions came to pass.

Italy, in fact, were one of the first teams to be officially eliminated from Rugby World Cup 2003, but they were very, very far from being one of the worst teams in the tournament. It is now a serious challenge for Italian rugby to put this scandal and their own disappointment firmly behind them. They did indeed unveil a new batch of talent, of which Sergio Parisse, the explosive young No. 8 not long out of his teens, was merely the talisman.

The pool had begun with a runaway victory by New Zealand, by 70-7 over an Italian team denuded by selection policy of all their top players. The match, played at Telstra Dome in Melbourne, produced some dazzling New Zealand running and eleven tries for the All Blacks against one by Italy.

Yet it was not all one-way traffic, because the untried Italian side often offered strong resistance, with Matteo Barbini and Andrea Masi in the centre particularly undaunted by the barrage of attacks that they had to face. And it was a disturbing day for New Zealand in another sense – they lost Tana Umaga, their influential centre, with a serious knee problem. They also replaced Joe Rokocoko, who threatened to be one of the stars of the tournament, after he picked up a less serious hamstring injury.

New Zealand's 11 tries comprised two each from Rokocoko, Carlos Spencer and Doug Howlett, and one apiece from Reuben Thorne, Brad Thorn, Justin Marshall, Leon MacDonald and Dan Carter. Carter, taking over the kicking duties from Carlos Spencer, managed six conversions and was highly influential in general play. New Zealand gained the first bonus point in the history of World Cup rugby when they notched up their fourth try – and this before the half-time whistle. Italy passed up several try-scoring chances with a lack of steadiness as the line approached, but they did score when Matt Phillips made a determined,

bullocking charge. It is Italy's misfortune that they always seem to be drawn in the same group as New Zealand, and their progress as a rugby nation will be confirmed only when they feel able to field a top team against the All Blacks, rather than effectively conceding the game and trying to limit the damage.

Melbourne was also the venue for the next match in Pool D, and it was a thoroughly disappointing affair. The Welsh victory over Canada by 41 points to 10 revealed that the Canadians had dipped further from their magnificent height in the 1991 World Cup, when they reached the quarter-finals and took New Zealand all the way in a wonderful match played in Lille, northern France. That kind of form was something of a distant memory as the privations of lack of funding and impossible logistics begin to hit home. Wales, never really getting out of first gear, scored five tries

BELOW **New Zealand centre and vice-captain Tana Umaga in action against Italy before an accidental collision with team-mate Carlos Spencer resulted in his suffering a cruciate ligament injury.**

ABOVE **Gareth Thomas steps inside Ryan Smith on his way to score in the dying moments of Wales's 41-10 win over Canada. Iestyn Harris converted, as he did his side's four other tries.**

to one, but there was a ragged air about proceedings. Sonny Parker, Mark Jones, Gareth Cooper, Colin Charvis and Gareth Thomas scored tries for Wales, and Kevin Tkachuk registered the single Canadian reply. However, Josh Jackson looked a fine new player for Canada, while Bobby Ross, the Canadian fly half, played cleverly and also added a dropped goal.

The chief Welsh attacking weapon in a humdrum display that lacked pace and bite was probably the passing in midfield of Iestyn Harris, the former rugby league star, who had finally settled down in the inside centre position. No one would call Harris a powerhouse, but his long, lobbed passes did make space for the Welsh wide players, although they often came hair-raisingly close

to being intercepted. This early match left Wales in urgent need of improvement and left Canada in urgent need of some kind of consolation.

Italy rediscovered themselves emphatically in Canberra in the next Pool D game when they wheeled out all their big guns and defeated Tonga 36-12. Denis Dallan, one of the most industrious and inventive wings in the whole tournament, scored two tries for Italy, with Manuel Dallan, his brother, crossing for the other.

Significantly, there were also 21 points from Rima Wakarua, the New Zealand-born fly half who had been drafted in late to the Italian squad after qualifying through residence. Kirwan had been criticised for discarding Ramiro Pez, the incumbent fly half who was judged good enough to sign for Leicester. Wakarua was hardly a dazzling attacking force, but his steadiness and his expert goal-kicking were major pluses for Italy. The Azzurri were also well served by the promising Parisse and by Andrea Lo

Cicero, one of the most difficult props in the competition, who caused the Tongan scrum no end of grief. Tonga did score tries through centre John Payne and wing Tevita Tu'ifua, and they had superb players in Benhur Kivalu in the forwards and in Sililo Martens at scrum half. But they lost Inoke Afeaki, their captain, to injury. Everyone knows that a Tongan team with all its players at the disposal of the coach and with the proper preparation would be a match for most. But in common with too many teams in RWC 2003 Tonga were shorn of players and of funds, and it was hardly a surprise that they subsided to the bottom of the pool.

BELOW **All Black hooker Mark Hammett gets an unorthodox view of the world as he is upended by his Canadian counterpart, Aaron Abrams, at Telstra Dome.**

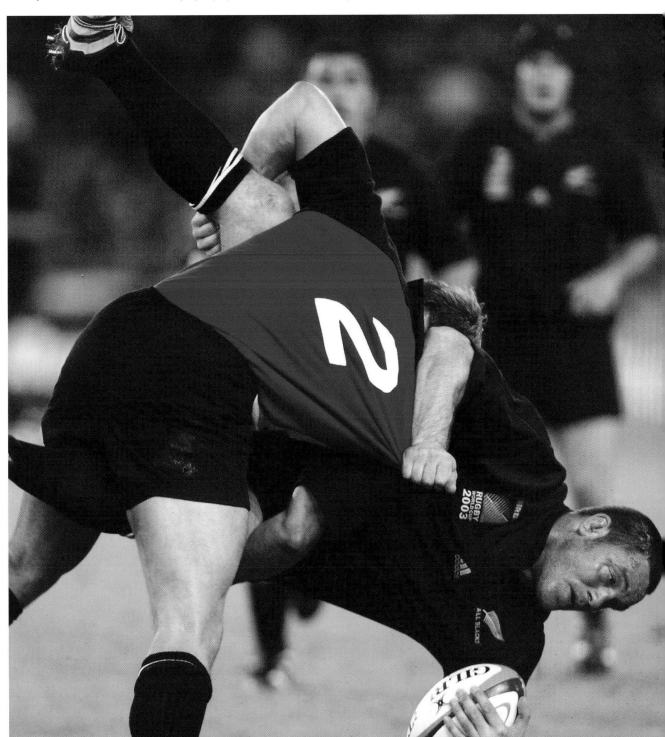

2003

New Zealand next had another assignment in Melbourne, sweeping aside a weakened Canada 68-6. Again, the Canadians resisted stoutly and it seemed at one stage that they might even hold New Zealand to no more than 50 points, until a late New Zealand rush finally buried them.

Canada's only points came from Jared Barker's boot, while New Zealand scored ten tries, four of them from the talented Mils Muliaina. His quartet provided the most striking memory of a fast-moving match. The remaining tries came from Rodney So'oialo (two), Caleb Ralph (two), Ma'a Nonu and Kees Meeuws. It was nothing more than a run-out for New Zealand, although Canada would have been encouraged by the performance of their younger men.

Wales were again unimpressive in their next game, winning only 27-20 against Tonga in heavy rain in Canberra. But the weather was no real excuse, since Welsh players are hardly unused to appearing in wet weather. Tonga played with great courage, but, once more, there was very little real power and pace in the Welsh game, and Tonga's late revival even put into question a Welsh victory.

Tonga scored three tries against two by Wales, with Pierre Hola, Heamani Lavaka and Benhur Kivalu all crossing. The Welsh scorers were Gareth Cooper and Martyn Williams, and Stephen Jones kicked four penalties and a conversion. There seemed few seeds visible of the splendid Welsh performance to come against New Zealand on this fitfully entertaining, but often rather grim, Canberra afternoon.

There was no respite for Italy because they had to play the determined Canadians only four days before they were to meet Wales in the key match. Italy had to find some way of winning while expending minimal energy and sustaining no serious injuries, and understandably they made hard work of it. They won 19-14 and were obviously delighted to sneak out ahead in a tough match, but onlookers realised that to back up this performance inside four days would be next to impossible. Canada were simply not in the mood to allow Italy to walk all over them.

Parisse scored Italy's try, with Wakarua adding a conversion and four penalties. Alessandro Troncon was in superb form for Italy, although a lack of concentration and the fact that their minds were probably on a future match did not show Italy in their best light. For Canada, who gave a much-improved performance,

LEFT **Italian centre Manuel Dallan hacks on against Canada at Canberra. This was a must-win encounter for the Azzurri if they were to have any chance of progressing to the quarter-finals. In the end they held on 19-14.**

RIGHT **Tonga fly half Pierre Hola's late-match challenge on Canada's skipper Al Charron. Charron, the veteran of four World Cups and playing his last international, was carried off with a facial injury.**

there was a memorable try from full back Quentin Fyffe. It was a job done for Italy, but as John Kirwan pointed out later, their build-up for the Welsh game, one of the most important matches in Italian rugby history, would consist of little more than rest.

New Zealand's 91-7 victory over Tonga was something of a formality and, indeed, one of those matches where you really want to avert the eyes as the tries piled up. Pierre Hola did add some kind of levity to the proceedings with a breakaway try for Tonga, but by then New Zealand had touched down 13 times. The scoreline was given a lopsided look by the fact that the All Blacks, remarkably for a team not judged to be a class kicking unit, managed to goal all 13 tries. The try scorers were Caleb Ralph (two), Mils Muliaina (two), Doug Howlett (two), Daniel Braid, Corey Flynn, Daniel Carter, Kees Meeuws, Leon MacDonald, Carlos Spencer and a penalty try. Frankly, the only area of real contest came when the teams fronted up for their war dances. Apart from that, New Zealand were simply too good, too fast and far too professional.

The next game in the pool saw Italy's 27-15 defeat as they gave a bedraggled and exhausted performance against Wales. But before the sumptuous final feast, we had another treat, with Canada and Tonga meeting in Wollongong as the two teams in the group without a victory. Understandably, it was a compelling and ferocious contest, with Canada always likely winners. Indeed, Canada's rapid improvement as the tournament progressed illustrated yet again the fact that proper preparation time can galvanise a team. It is just that Canada had neither the resources nor the time to indulge in proper preparation until they actually gathered in Australia for the big event itself.

The final score was 24-7, with Canada scoring tries through Sean Fauth and Aaron Abrams against one for Tonga from their superb captain, Inoke Afeaki. There was a disturbing note at the end of the match when Pierre Hola appeared to strike Al Charron with a sickening illegal shoulder charge. The Canadian captain was to recover after being carried off apparently senseless and after having 18 stitches. Hola escaped sanction, which seemed ridiculous. It was also a painfully inappropriate end for the mighty Charron. He has been one of the great players on the world rugby scene for a decade and more and typified the graft, sacrifice and sportsmanship of Canadian rugby. He deserved to walk off into a well-merited retirement, but his contribution to the game will be remembered far longer than will Hola's charge.

The scene was set for the titanic battle b...
and Wales, which ended with New ...
but proceeding to what the ...

Mils Muliaina (NZL) – four tries v Canada.

What they said...

Rima Wakarua – 50 points for Italy.

Italy: John Kirwan (coach)

❝We came into the event with a culture of losing. We are reversing that culture. We missed out on the quarters by inches. The schedule did us no favours, with all our games being crammed into two weeks. The structure should be fairer.❞

Canada: Winston Stanley (wing)

❝After three defeats we ended our tournament with a great win. After our captain, Al Charron, was stretchered off, we said: 'Ten more minutes for Al'.❞

Tonga: Jim Love (coach)

❝We felt like second-class citizens, being made to fly home less than eight hours after being eliminated. If the IRB does not do something about it, maybe we should not bother to come in future. Like Italy the draw was stacked against us with only 14 days to play our four games. Bringing our team together is impossible because they are scattered round the world.❞

New Zealand: Reuben Thorne (captain)

❝I hoped for a real battle after some easy wins, but the result against Wales was too close for comfort.❞

Wales: Colin Charvis (captain)

❝We are very proud of what we have achieved. We knew after our first two games that we had to step up a bit to perform against the New Zealanders. That's what we aimed for and that's what we did.❞

After a horrendous year, including a Six Nations whitewash, Welsh skipper Colin Charvis claims his side can take great heart from reaching the last eight.

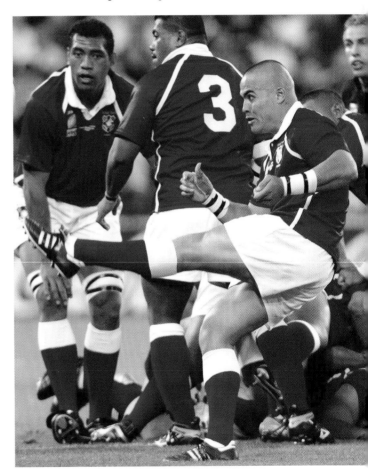

Sililo Martens – superb for Tonga.

QUARTER-FINAL
New Zealand v South Africa

BRENDAN GALLAGHER

South Africa against New Zealand is always the most mouthwatering of prospects, doubly so in a World Cup, and this game at Telstra Dome in Melbourne was to prove no exception. Twice the teams had encountered each other in the competition before and twice the Springboks had come out on top. The All Blacks were determined to reverse that trend against their bitterest of enemies.

Going into the game, South Africa were in good heart and appeared to have every chance. They were coming off an excellent 60-10 win over Samoa in Brisbane, a game in which their pack really clicked and crushed the life out of the Samoans. It came at a cost, though, with brilliant young flanker Joe Van Niekerk having to fly back to South Africa to have surgery on an anterior cruciate knee ligament injury.

It was a cruel blow to one of the emerging stars of the tournament, and though the Boks made brave noises about the opportunity of using the power and strength of Danie Rossouw, the absence of 'Big Joe' fatally undermined the balance of their back row.

There was optimism around, though, earlier in the week. Coach Rudi Straeuli spoke of the need for time and patience with his new team and how, given another year, they would definitely be world-beaters. 'Already today, they are capable of beating any side in a one-off game,' claimed Straeuli. 'But if South Africa shows faith in this squad and sticks with it they will have a team to take the country forward.'

Straeuli, under immense pressure before the tournament after a bad run of results and the allegations of racism within the squad which resulted in the setting up of the King Inquiry, insisted that his presence at the helm was immaterial. He was not coaching South Africa for personal ambition; he was coaching because there was an important job to be done and he was honoured to be overseeing the future of the national side.

The squad arrived from Brisbane in a relaxed frame of mind, and that atmosphere remained. For one player it was a very special week. Veteran scrum half Joost van der Westhuizen had already announced that he was to retire from international rugby

RIGHT **Springbok wing Ashwin Willemse rises to claim the ball ahead of his New Zealand opposite number, Joe Rokocoko, and full back Mils Muliaina.**

Second XV. It wasn't, but the perception was that the All Blacks had badly underperformed against a side they should have made short work of.

New Zealand did what they always do in such circumstances and cranked everything up in training, especially in defence, where large holes had appeared the week before when Wales's ability to either chip behind the defence or take defenders on had the alarm bells ringing.

In midweek there were vague hints that Tana Umaga could yet complete a miracle return from his posterior cruciate injury,

the moment South Africa were eliminated, and though he obviously hoped that would be later rather than sooner the possibility had to be addressed. He was determined to enjoy every moment and savour every last day in the squad before stepping down.

New Zealand, meanwhile, arrived back at their Melbourne base camp smarting just a little after receiving an unexpectedly hard time from what some people dismissively called a Wales

ABOVE **Rising star Joe Van Niekerk suffered knee ligament damage in South Africa's final pool game against Samoa, and his absence left a big hole to fill in the Springbok back row.**
RIGHT **All Black Tana Umaga also had knee problems from the first match with Italy. Though there was speculation he might return, the centre spent the match on the side lines.**

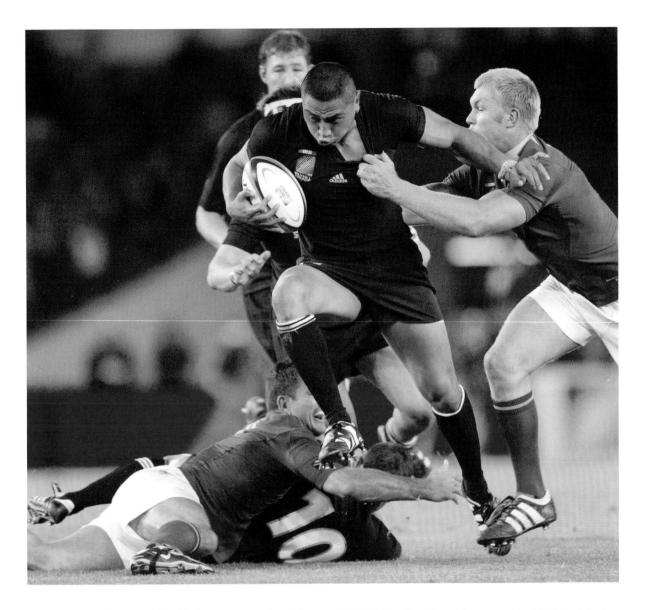

and the team doctor, John Mayhew, spoke about the extraordinary genetic qualities that make islanders able to recover more quickly from such injuries. Mayhew might have been correct, but ultimately New Zealand decided not to risk their vice-captain and key midfield back.

Their other key injury concern was No. 8 Jerry Collins, who had damaged rib cartilages in the match against Wales. Normally you would expect a two- or three-week lay-off, but Collins was determined to play – and how! He proved to be an inspiration on the night.

So it was off to Telstra Dome. It was not a packed house – a tad over 42,000 fans attending, mainly from New Zealand – and for the first half an eerie silence enveloped the stadium. Whether

ABOVE **What's a rib cartilage injury among friends? All Black No. 8 Jerry Collins, who incurred the damage against Wales, rampages all over South Africa just a week later.**

the fans were waiting to be impressed or the game simply did not engross them was not entirely clear, but as an occasion the match only really took off after the break.

Or perhaps it was because from the very beginning there seemed to be only one side in it. New Zealand's pack – often much maligned, especially the front five – took the game by the scruff of the neck and never relinquished their grip. South Africa were on the back foot from minute one and were never able to gain enough possession to secure any kind of bridgehead.

The first half ended with a classic wipe-out tackle from Collins, clearly feeling no ill effects from the ribs, on poor Thinus Delport, who was nearly sent back to Gloucester with the force of the impact. 'It was like being hit by a brick shithouse,' was his apt comment when questioned later. If nothing else, it demonstrated that New Zealand had the ascendancy overwhelmingly when it came to the physical confrontations.

Initially the points did not come in a rush, though a glorious 60-yard break from Carlos Spencer created a try under the posts for Leon MacDonald, who added the conversion and two penalties. South Africa kept in touch with a brace of penalties from young Derick Hougaard, but the writing was on the wall. New Zealand were attacking from all angles and should have scored two or three more tries before the break, the most notable miss coming from Joe Rokocoko, who unaccountably decided to go on the inside when a trademark outside burn would have seen a clear overlap converted into five points.

ABOVE **Twenty-year-old Springbok stand-off Derick Hougaard, headgear discarded for kicking duties, slots one of his three penalties in the match.**
RIGHT **For my next trick… Master magician Carlos Spencer on the attack again. The crowd-pleasing fly half was at the top of his form against South Africa.**

After the break, New Zealand were more clinical, and as the game developed, the wonderfully entertaining Spencer began to reveal his full bag of tricks, notably his clever over-the-shoulder passes when running in the opposite direction and his clever kicks off the wrong side of the foot. The crowd loved it and began to respond. When in the right mood, Spencer is a master of his craft and hugely entertaining.

After an initial early scare when South Africa should have scored a try right after the break, New Zealand began to put the game beyond doubt. Aaron Mauger kicked a dropped goal, and Keven Mealamu, who a year earlier had struggled to secure a Super 12 contract, powered past four defenders to barge over for a popular try and enhance his reputation as one of the world's best hookers.

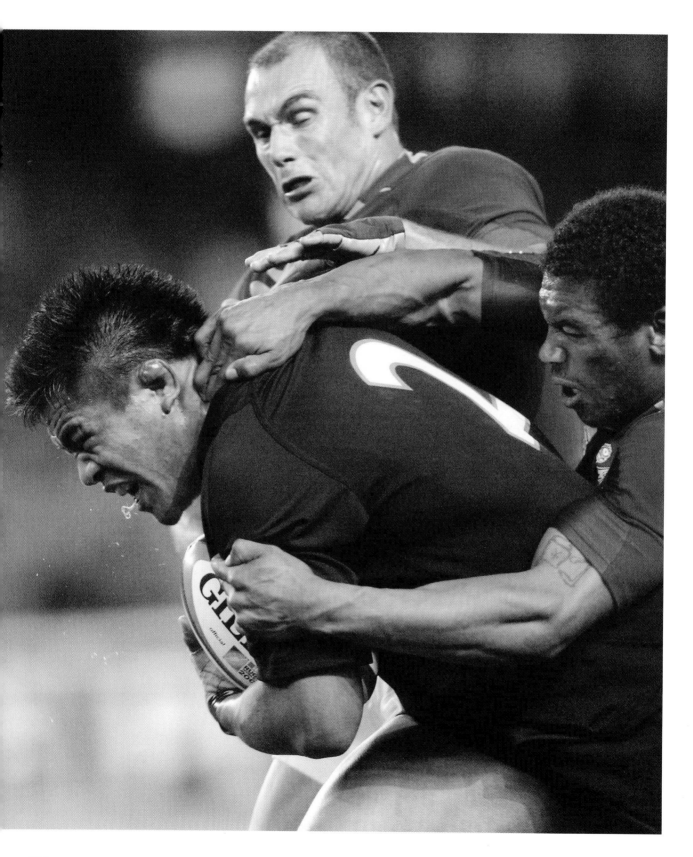

Then came the moment that everybody will remember and talk about – New Zealand's third try, which came about as a direct result of a brilliant, intuitive through-the-legs pass from Spencer to Rokocoko, who scored in the corner. It appeared to have come straight from the Fijian sevens coaching manual and would have been fairly outrageous on a beery Sunday afternoon at the Hong Kong Sevens. To pull off such a stroke in a World Cup quarter-final against South Africa almost defied belief.

It was no accident or fluke, however, as wing Doug Howlett, a colleague of Spencer with both the Blacks and Auckland,

explained later: 'He is a little maestro with every trick in the trade and it's great fun playing outside him. He is just the same in training; he is always perfecting his tricks so after a while you get to recognise the signs and guess what's coming up. We

FACING PAGE **Keven Mealamu powers to the line to score New Zealand's second try despite the attentions of Ashwin Willemse and full back Jaco van der Westhuyzen.**
BELOW **It's that man Joe again. Joe Rokocoko converts Carlos Spencer's cheeky through-the-legs pass into a try in the corner.**

communicate a lot so some of the ploys are not quite off the cuff. But even then he will try and throw in something different. Half the fun is trying to think like he thinks.'

It was the crowning glory to Spencer's own personal performance and indeed the match. As a contest, it did not live up to expectations. We believed the Boks would pose a bigger threat up front and that the physical challenge would be greater. It did not work out like that, probably because New Zealand were too good to allow that to happen.

Though the crowd were still purring after Spencer's second-half antics, New Zealand coach John Mitchell did not seem overdelighted with victory, taking time out to identify the faults in New Zealand's performance at the post-match press conference.

Mitchell, who often resorts to computer talk at press conferences in a strange attempt to render them void of emotion, then came up with his classic 'There is only a small window to enjoy such performances', which soon became one of the quotes of the tournament as it was beamed around the world. His attitude sometimes seems diametrically opposed to that of some of his all-singing, all-dancing backs, but it works for New Zealand, so who are we to complain?

The press conference also saw an emotional exit from Joost van der Westhuizen, who thanked everybody for being allowed to be part of the world game. It was a nice sentiment from Joost, but in truth it is us who must be thanking him. He was a warrior from start to finish for South Africa and the inspiration for so many of their victories. It was Joost who was first out of the trenches in the 1995 World Cup final and made the first big tackle on Jonah Lomu to show that he was human – this despite the fact that the scrum half was playing with two broken ribs.

Before the crippling knee injuries began to take their toll, van der Westhuizen was unbelievably quick, and his 40- to 50-yard blind-side breaks became the trademark of his game. His speed came from an early love of sevens, and there are those who will tell you that his greatest ever individual performance was at the 1997 World Sevens final, when he appeared to take on the mighty Fijians virtually single-handed. What's more, he didn't lose by much!

'It's been an honour and a privilege and now I just want to away and be one big happy, happy family man,' said Joost afterwards. 'I will miss it very badly. Nothing can replace the honour of representing your country, standing in a line before the game and listening to the anthems and thinkng that you do all this for the people you love. It is very humbling. I am so glad I was given the opportunity to enjoy a life in sport. It was the luckiest break of my life.'

His last contribution, and one of his most valuable, was to recover from injury one more time and help nurse a very young Springboks squad through some difficult times and a testing tournament. He passed on the baton as to exactly what it means to be a Springbok and a World Cup winner.

Overall South Africa did not do so bad. A 25-6 defeat against England was not very flattering – they played much better than that – but there were signs in the remaining pool games of good times ahead. Despite the disappointment of defeat, South African

rugby advanced considerably during the tournament, and manager Gideon Sam, a dignified figure throughout, immediately called for continuity as they looked further to the future.

'We must not stuff up this time,' replied Rhian Oberholzer, chief executive of the South African Rugby Union. 'Ten coaches in 11 years, or is it 11 coaches in 10 years? It is too many. We must take a leaf out of the RFU book and plan properly for the future. There are good players to work with and Rudi Straeuli has been appointed coach through to 2005.'

As for New Zealand, they marched on to the semi-finals in good shape and in much better heart than after their win over Wales. The forwards had stood up to be counted, and the backs finally achieved a little more fluency. With Australia to come, the scene was well and truly set.

BELOW AND FOLLOWING PAGE **Joost van der Westhuizen calls time on a golden career after 89 Tests. He captained his country eight times, scored 38 Test tries and was a World Cup winner in 1995.**

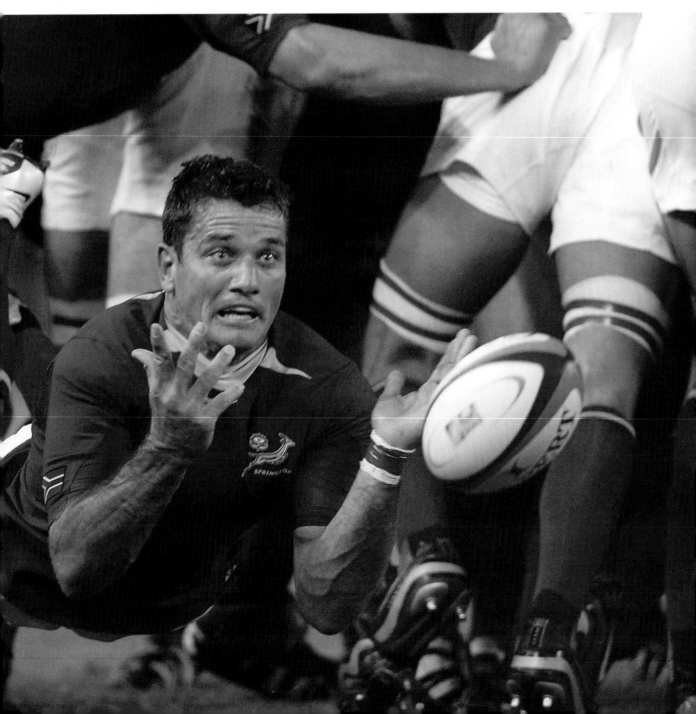

Leon MacDonald (NZL) – 16 points.

What they said...

South Africa: Joost van der Westhuizen (scrum half)

❝The real sadness for me is losing again to the All Blacks, not that my life at the base of the Springbok scrum stops here and now. I'll now be a TV analyst and a family man.❞

Joost brings down the curtain on his decade-long Test-match career.

South Africa: Gideon Sam (manager)

❝The youth in this team is exciting. We must not keep chopping and changing. Stability is unquestionable.❞

South Africa's manager wants an end to uncertainty.

John Mitchell – New Zealand coach.

Gideon Sam – South Africa manager.

New Zealand: John Mitchell (coach)

❝There is nothing better for a traditional New Zealander than to beat the Springboks. There is something unique about it. Our pack stamped it's authority on the game and we knew that we were going to be in a long, hard grind and that's the way the game worked out, but we have gone one more win up in a very special contest between our two nations.❞

Perfect delivery every time.

No-matter how tough your delivery challenge, **TNT Express** can handle it. Our commitment to providing the fastest and most reliable national and international delivery services for business means we're ready to tackle anything.

TNT Express

QUARTER-FINAL
Australia v Scotland

JILL DOUGLAS

rash, bang, wallop signalled the end of Scotland's World Cup campaign. The crash was a high ball thudding into fly half Chris Paterson's head in the warm-up. The bang was the explosive start from the Scots to silence the Wallabies in the first 40 minutes of their quarter-final at Brisbane's Suncorp Stadium. And the wallop was the three tries in 20 minutes from Australia that snuffed out any chance of the Scots causing the biggest upset in the tournament's history. But this was a brave effort from the Scots, and a much-improved performance on their four pool matches because this group of players felt they had a

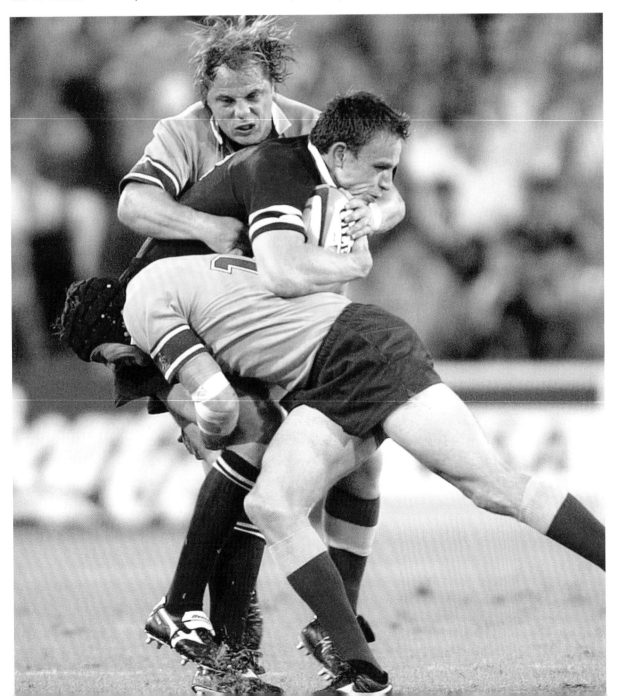

ABOVE **Wendell Sailor comes barrelling up to support Mat Rogers as he is hauled down by the Scottish defence. These two plus Lote Tuqiri formed an all ex-rugby league back three for Australia.**
PREVIOUS PAGE **Crash, bang, wallop! Flanker Phil Waugh and fly half Stephen Larkham stop Scotland's Andrew Henderson in his tracks.**
FACING PAGE **Wagga Wagga-born Scotland lock Nathan Hines takes the high ground at the line out.**

point to prove. The day before the match the Brisbane *Courier-Mail* printed an article describing the Scots' trip to Australia as 'the tour from hell'. It suggested that when the players entered the stadium, it would be the culmination of weeks of controversy, infighting, allegations of misbehaviour and a breakdown of relations between the team and the travelling media.

There is no doubt that there were problems between the press and the team after the reaction to Scotland's opening match of the tournament against Japan. But this was a tight group of players who had been through some difficult times together, and they wanted more than anything else to show their critics that they could compete on rugby's biggest stage.

The heroics of Ireland and Wales against Australia and New Zealand were a source of inspiration for the Scots as they prepared to meet the reigning world champions in Brisbane. And a group of pipers in the city's botanical gardens also gave the team a timely boost. The Pipes and Drums of the Queensland Police Band had been booked months earlier for their regular performance in the beautiful surroundings of the gardens and it coincided with a line-out session with the Scottish pack. It was a

surreal moment as Gordon Bulloch put the big men through their paces to the sound of 'Killiecrankie'. And as the players completed their training, prop Bruce Douglas, an accomplished piper, gave the police band a blast of 'Scotland the Brave'.

Indeed they would need to be at their very bravest if they were to give the Australians a game on Saturday night. If the Scots thought they had taken some flak, they needed only to pick up a newspaper to see they weren't alone. The Australian public demanded success, and there was a general feeling that the Wallabies so far hadn't produced the kind of rugby the country expected. The chief executive of the Australian Rugby Union, John O'Neill, had even lost patience, declaring that it was 'time to deliver' on the big salaries and investment made in the team.

Much of the criticism centred on Jones's selection. Too many old heads, no consistency and uncompetitive in the line out – the knives were being sharpened if the Wallabies failed to put in a big

ABOVE **Scotland stand-off Chris Paterson is helped to his feet after being felled by an incoming rugby ball during the warm-up.**
RIGHT **Paterson, recovered, brings down Wallaby danger man Fijian-born left wing Lote Tuqiri.**

performance in the quarter-final. But Eddie Jones is no fool and surely had one eye already on a semi-final against the All Blacks, so was fine-tuning his line-up in anticipation.

He stayed true to Stephen Larkham and captain George Gregan as half backs but finally seemed to be listening to his critics by bringing in Lote Tuqiri for Joe Roff, and injury meant he could call on Stirling Mortlock for Matt Burke, who had failed to impress so far.

Much was expected of Australia's back-three rugby league converts, Tuqiri, Mat Rogers and Wendell Sailor. But Jones was forced into a change in the pack when David Giffin suffered an injury in training. Justin Harrison stepped into the starting line-up, with Daniel Vickerman taking his place on the bench.

Scotland put out their strongest team available, though with no proven open-side flanker now left in the squad could they handle one of the most dynamic back rows in the business? Ian

McGeechan kept faith with Chris Paterson at stand-off, who partnered Bryan Redpath at half back in what would be the latter's final game for Scotland if it ended in defeat.

Paterson, however, was fortunate to play a part in this match at all after suffering a heavy blow to the head in the warm-up. Fifteen minutes before kick-off a high ball hit him solidly on the temple and he was knocked to the ground. There were worried looks all around as he was led unsteadily to the medical room. Anxious moments for McGeechan and Co., but thankfully Paterson recovered enough to take to the field, though he afterwards admitted he had been knocked out cold.

Prince Harry was in the crowd as the anthems were sung, and this week there was no twitching for Marty Leslie, just a steely determination from this squad of Scots. The Wallabies took an early lead through an Elton Flatley penalty, but the Scotland side must have been heartened by the nervy handling of the Australian

backs. The Wallabies played to their wings and enjoyed scoring opportunities, only for the last pass to let them down. In one incident, Lote Tuqiri came off his left wing to burst through the midfield and put Mat Rogers in at the corner, only for Rogers to fumble the ball and knock on the easiest of passes. Tuqiri always looked dangerous, and a cover tackle from Chris Paterson in the first five minutes stopped an almost certain try and proved the young fly half had been revived from his earlier bang on the head. Indeed the Scottish defence was magnificent throughout, and Australia looked rattled as they held firm.

PREVIOUS PAGES **Sixteen and a half stones on the hoof. Flanker Cameron Mather, Scotland's outstanding forward on the night, mounts an upfield charge.**
BELOW **Centre Stirling Mortlock caps a 60-metre dash with a spectacular dive under the posts to register Australia's first try.**

Flatley and Paterson traded penalties and the score was 9-6 after 36 minutes, then Paterson dropped the sweetest of goals from 50 metres out to make it all square at the break. The Gala stand-off played with composure and maturity throughout the match, and his performance prompted Wallaby great Mark Ella to remark that he was 'one of the sweetest kickers in the game'.

Scotland had had their own opportunities – Kenny Logan looked to be in at the corner when Gregor Townsend kicked a beautifully weighted cross-pitch ball, only for referee Steve Walsh to bring them back for a Scottish penalty. Wendell Sailor reacted to a hand in his face by slapping the Australian-born second-rower Nathan Hines. Walsh penalised the Australians but should have sin-binned the former rugby league man.

It was a gutsy performance from Scotland in that first half, and it was reflected in the statistics – Scotland had had 50 per cent of the possession but 62 per cent of the territory. In the lead-up

to the game Bryan Redpath said the Scots had to keep their half of the field clean and play the game in the Wallabies' territory, and it was a tactic that kept Scotland very much in the match and silenced the Australian fans for 40 minutes at Suncorp Stadium.

Clearly the Australians had to make changes, and in the second half they brought on the 6ft 6ins Matt Cockbain for George Smith to broaden their limited line-out options. Nine-all then at the restart and all pressure on the Aussies – the team to score first would be given a huge psychological advantage.

Sadly for the Scots, it was the Wallabies who notched up the all-important first try from a turnover, Phil Waugh feeding Flatley, then Harrison, who swept a high pass to Stirling Mortlock, who raced almost 60 metres to touch down under the posts. So 16-9 five minutes into the second period.

The pressure on Scotland was increased with a Flatley penalty, and it continued when Waugh capitalised on a loose ball

from a Scottish line out. The danger man Tuqiri raced cross-field, and at the ruck the Wallabies won quick ball for George Gregan, who kicked ahead to score. A sweet moment for the Australian captain, who had been under so much pressure in the build-up to this match but who had now put the match beyond the Scots. The scoreline read 26-9 with only the last quarter to play. And if there was any doubt about the result, David Lyons made sure of it with a pick and drive, bulldozing through the Scots to take the score to 33-9.

After their stirring performance, however, no one at Suncorp Stadium would have begrudged the battling Scotland team a try. It came in the final moments as substitute Rob Russell, replacing Gordon Bulloch at hooker, charged over from a line out with

BELOW **Wallaby skipper George Gregan pounces on his own kick ahead to touch down for his side's second score.**

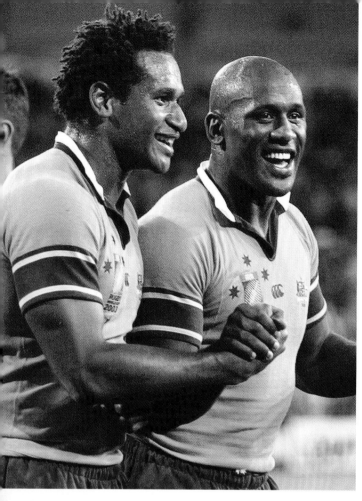

stand-out forward Cameron Mather supporting him. It was ironic, however, that the Scots' only try came from the Australian-born hooker, supported by the Kiwi-born Mather.

The full-time whistle brought emotional scenes as it signalled not only the end of Scotland's World Cup dream but also the end of an era. Jim Telfer, one of the game's greatest servants, was stepping down from his role as assistant coach and Scotland's director of rugby. 'I'm looking forward to retiring; it frees me from the pressure and from the straitjacket. I am looking forward to doing other things and travel is high on that agenda,' said Telfer, who will be replaced as director of rugby by Ian McGeechan. Telfer was rightly proud of the Scots' efforts, saying it was one of the best forward displays he had seen in recent years. But he was critical of Steve Walsh's decision to allow the Australians' first try, disappointed that Waugh had not been penalised in the lead-up.

The match also brought captain Bryan Redpath's international career to a close. 'I'm disappointed not to have won the match but I couldn't have asked for more from this group of players. It has been an excellent tournament, certainly the best World Cup I have been involved in.

'The support we have had has been second to none,' said Redpath. 'That's credit to those out here and the ex-pats. It was probably better than at home. They made it very special for me and I've enjoyed my 10 years.'

Wasps winger Kenny Logan also called time on his international rugby career, 11 years after making his debut against Australia. Seventy caps for the former Stirling County winger. He too has served the Scottish cause well.

And so Scotland's World Cup quest came to an end – a mixed campaign but a positive finale in Brisbane. We saw the blossoming of Chris Paterson at half back and the emergence of the strong-running Simon Danielli on the wing. There was also confirmation that Simon Taylor is a world-class rugby player.

Lessons will have been learned, and there is no doubt the incoming coach, Matt Williams, will have his own ideas about preparing for France in 2007. He may have listened to his countryman Eddie Jones ahead of this quarter-final. The Australia coach said, 'This World Cup won't be won by the team playing the most adventurous rugby. It will be won by the team who play the smartest rugby.' On 8 November at Suncorp Stadium, sadly for the Scots, the smart rugby was played by the Wallabies.

ABOVE LEFT AND LEFT **Elation and dejection. Lote Tuqiri and Wendell Sailor celebrate, while Scotland must swallow the bitter pill. For Kenny Logan (centre) it is disappointment mixed with the emotion of his farewell to the international stage.**

Simon Danielli (SCO) – an exciting new talent.

What they said...

Australia: Eddie Jones (coach)

"We have had criticism of players and selection. But we keep proving them wrong. But I admit that we have to improve to retain that cup. Against Scotland we had bad trouble in the line out, dropped lots of ball, but still defended well. Then we came out and put the match to bed."

The Australia coach acknowledges the knockers.

Bryan Redpath – Scotland captain.

Eddie Jones – Australia coach.

Scotland: Bryan Redpath (captain)

"I've had a great ten years. Now I'll watch and try not to criticise."

The Scotland captain retires from international rugby.

Scotland: Ian McGeechan (coach)

"I am very proud of our displays. In the final match against Australia we produced a wonderful forward effort, especially in the line out, where we completely commanded."

Scotland: Jim Telfer (assistant coach)

"We'll get more credibility back home after the rubbishing we have had to put up with."

QUARTER-FINAL
France v Ireland

JIM NEILLY

ABOVE **French wing Aurelien Rougerie tries to get round Ireland's John Kelly as Les Bleus outgun the Irish to proceed to the semi-finals of the World Cup for the third successive time.**

The look on Keith Wood's face said it all. Long before the final whistle sounded at Melbourne's Telstra Dome, everyone, including Ireland's inspirational captain, knew that Ireland's World Cup quest and Wood's distinguished career were over. Wood, leading Ireland for the 36th time, embraced his opposite number, Fabien Galthie of France, knowing that had circumstances been reversed it would have been Galthie announcing his retirement at the close of an equally illustrious international odyssey.

For Wood, who had defied all the odds to reach his third World Cup, it was a doubly bitter blow given the genuine belief in the Irish camp that, following victory against Argentina and the narrowest of losses to Australia, they could record a fourth win in five games against France and qualify for the World Cup semi-finals for the first time. But despite a spirited second-half performance by Ireland, the French played with such pace and aggression that the game was over as a contest well before the interval, and Ireland, who had been quietly revelling in their IRB

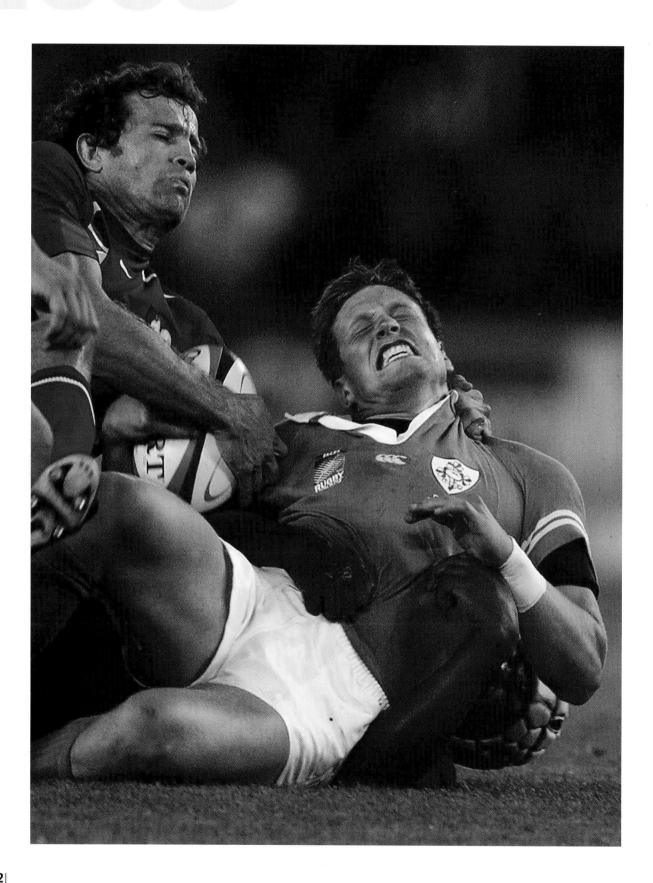

ABOVE **Brian O'Driscoll takes to the air in an attempt to reel in French centre Tony Marsh. The Kiwi-born Marsh was happily fit and healthy again in time for the World Cup after a battle against cancer.** FACING PAGE **Ronan O'Gara, who started at fly half ahead of David Humphreys, is scragged by Fabien Galthie and Serge Betsen.**

ranking, must have wondered if they had made any worthwhile progress in the four years since the ignominious defeat by Argentina in Lens.

In the immediate aftermath of a one-point loss to the Wallabies in the final game in Pool A, the Irish had pronounced themselves disappointed but nonetheless satisfied that, given eight days to prepare, they were more than capable of edging out France. Eddie O'Sullivan felt that the fact that France hadn't been tested, while his troops were battle hardened, would be crucial, and if Ireland could replicate the forward display that threatened to overwhelm Australia, a semi-final place was assured.

Ireland's preparations were tinged with sadness five days before the French game as the squad said farewells to both Alan Quinlan and Denis Hickie. Quinlan had dislocated his left shoulder scoring a crucial try against Argentina and had remained with the

party in order to allow the inflammation to subside, while Hickie, who suffered a ruptured Achilles tendon against Australia, needed to go home as soon as possible. The wing-threequarter, Ireland's top try scorer, underwent surgery within 24 hours of his return to Dublin, knowing that his entire season was a write-off; Quinlan, following minor shoulder reconstruction, was harbouring hopes of returning to action by the end of the season.

As had been the case with all Ireland's previous games, the balance between serious training and relaxation was achieved to

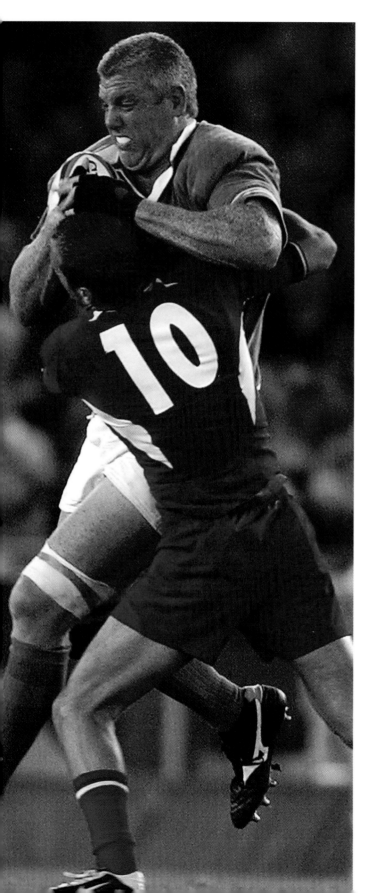

everyone's satisfaction, though the Irish squad were pleasantly surprised when a trip to a local swimming pool coincided with the arrival of a group of 30 air stewardesses who were receiving instruction in safety techniques in the event of an emergency landing on water. It appears that there was no shortage of brawny volunteers when it came to resuscitation techniques.

When it came to selection for the game with France, Eddie O'Sullivan, who had started fewer players in his opening three games than any other coach in the tournament, made two changes from the side that had played Australia. John Kelly replaced the unfortunate Denis Hickie on the left wing, having also done so after the latter was injured against the Wallabies, but O'Sullivan's decision to prefer Victor Costello to Anthony Foley at No. 8 was viewed with disapproval by most of the press corps.

LEFT **Little v large. In-form France stand-off Frederic Michalak gets to grips with Ireland No. 8 Victor Costello at Telstra Dome.**
BELOW **Serge Betsen (6) watches and waits for an opportunity to pounce as a scrum disintegrates on the Irish put-in.**

O'Sullivan had, since he succeeded Warren Gatland, named Foley as one of his vice-captains in every squad and had regularly extolled the Munsterman's qualities of leadership, intelligence and tactical knowledge. Since Foley had returned to the international fold for the game against Scotland in 2000, he had never been dropped in almost 40 Tests and had passed Willie Duggan's cap record for an Irish No. 8 (39).

For the first time during the campaign, O'Sullivan seemed tense at the team announcement, amid speculation that the omission of Foley might not have gone down well with Keith Wood. O'Sullivan's logic regarding Costello's qualities as a ball carrier was met with a fair degree of scepticism, although this selectorial departure served to deflect debate over the retention of Ronan O'Gara ahead of David Humphreys at out-half. France, ominously, had reverted to the starting XV that had crushed Scotland with ease, and Bernard Laporte was confident enough to precede O'Sullivan by 24 hours with his team announcement.

The massive hike in prices from the pool games meant that the crowd at Telstra Dome was well short of capacity. But while the Irish supporters by far outstripped French fans in terms of quantity and volume as the kick-off approached, they had to wait for almost an hour for a reason to enthuse, as France, with a display reminiscent of spring afternoons in Paris, served up an irresistible cocktail of pace, power and skill to which Ireland had no answer.

It took the French just three minutes to confirm that they really did have too much of everything for Ireland. Without the talents of Geordan Murphy and Denis Hickie to consider, the French, predictably, attacked Ireland's back three. With John Kelly, who looked ill at ease from the outset, involved on the right wing, Frederic Michalak launched a massive cross-kick towards the Irish left, where Girvan Dempsey found himself under pressure from three salivating Frenchmen, and Imanol Harinordoquy beat Ireland's full back to the high bounce.

New Zealand-born Tony Marsh, who had undergone major chemotherapy for testicular cancer just six months earlier, gathered Harinordoquy's tap-down, and the centre, despite a fine tackle from Peter Stringer, sent Olivier Magne, one of five

survivors from the 1999 final, in for the opening try. Michalak, in outstanding kicking form with an average of 25 points in his first three games, converted and also landed a penalty just after Aurelien Rougerie came close to getting his team's second try, putting France 10-0 up.

Ireland couldn't get started, with the French defence, epitomised by a series of big hits from flanker Serge Betsen, courting the offside line with precision; it was Betsen's collision, albeit an accidental one, with Ronan O'Gara that forced the Irish out-half from the field. When he returned, it was obvious that he was well short of complete composure. The French scrum, low and aggressive, disrupted Ireland's early put-ins, negating Costello's ability to pick and drive, and while Ireland managed to win their own line-out ball, they never pressurised the French as they had done the Pumas and the Wallabies at crucial times.

FACING PAGE **France No. 8 Imanol Harinordoquy celebrates as he prepares to touch down for his side's third try of the evening.**
BELOW **Four minutes earlier, flying machine Christophe Dominici had scorched home to notch France's second.**

At the line, France had just too many winning options, with Raphael Ibanez finding Harinordoquy, locks Fabien Pelous and Jerome Thion, and Magne (who moved up and down the line out at will), all to an extent that was light years from the shambles that the Wallabies had presented eight days earlier.

To Ireland's credit, they kept their discipline and clawed their way back into the game, but went further behind when a wild pass from O'Gara shot beyond the reach of Costello and Malcolm O'Kelly, leaving Shane Horgan to cope with a French back row who snaffled possession in an instant. Betsen unleashed Christophe Dominici, who outpaced Horgan for the try, which Michalak goaled with ease.

It got worse for Ireland. Galthie, luxuriating in the knowledge that Ireland were watching his half-back partner Michalak, a dozen years his junior, went on a run that belied his 34 years. He then fed prop Jean Jacques Crenca, who in turn gave a perfectly timed pass to the rampaging Harinordoquy and the No. 8 finished it off with a spectacular dive. Michalak converted and popped over a second penalty to leave Ireland stunned and trailing 27-0 at half-time.

Any notion that Ireland would get the early second-half boost they craved was dispelled from the restart as Michalak kicked his third penalty and converted a stroll-in try by Crenca, following

wonderful hands by Magne and Rougerie, to make it 37-0. As one wag remarked at that point, 'Jaysus lads, four quick tries and you're back in the game!'

Eddie O'Sullivan replaced O'Gara with Humphreys, and Reggie Corrigan with Marcus Horan, and the effect was almost instantaneous. The young Munster prop added an element of dynamism to Ireland's forward play, while Humphreys, winning

BELOW **Centre Kevin Maggs swerves and steps on the gas on his way to putting Ireland on the scoresheet with a try in the 53rd minute. David Humphreys converted.**

his 60th cap and playing like a man who had nothing to prove, shipped a lovely short pass to Kevin Maggs, who showed great pace and determination to burst fully 40 metres for a try which Humphreys converted. Humphreys, only the fourth Irish player to win 60 caps (after Mike Gibson, Willie John McBride and Fergus Slattery), then watched Michalak kick his fourth penalty before he slid a kick through the French defence from 15 metres out and saw Brian O'Driscoll beat several defenders to the touchdown.

Raphael Ibanez, France's 1999 World Cup captain, winning his 70th cap, was in the sin-bin at the time, and, like his colleagues, was relieved when Michalak kicked his fifth penalty for a 43-14 lead. But Ireland finished strongly, and replacement scrum half Guy Easterby, after several phases, released O'Driscoll, who had to work hard to twist and writhe through would-be tacklers for his second try, which Humphreys converted with full-time beckoning. It was a face-saving finale as far as the scoreboard went, but the nightmare of the first 50 minutes will be relived for some time.

A tearful Keith Wood gave his post-match interview with typical candour, but he spoke of his disappointment about an Irish display that scarcely reflected the efforts made by all concerned during the tournament. Eddie O'Sullivan gathered the entire squad and ancillary staff in a circle for a few words of praise and solidarity, before leaving the field through a double line of Frenchmen, a gesture reminiscent of a bygone era.

Wood was applauded into the post-match press conference, where he announced that he would never play again, at any level. O'Sullivan paid a fine tribute to his captain, describing him as 'a genuine rugby legend'. For his part, Wood said that while he had experienced many highs during his ten-season career, including a winning series with the 1997 Lions to South Africa, playing for his country had meant most to him. He made special mention of

BELOW **Brian O'Driscoll gets the touchdown despite the efforts of half the French back division. The Leinster centre's two tries late in the game helped to give the Ireland score some respectability.**

ABOVE **Passing into legend. Keith Wood with Fabien Galthie at no-side. 'One of us was going to retire straight after this game,' said Wood, 'and we both knew it.'**

Ian Bayley, the surgeon who had operated on his right shoulder a number of times to enable him to return, time and again, to play in the most physically demanding of positions.

The Irish captain spoke, too, of the respect he had for Fabien Galthie of France and that he felt that there was nobody more worthy of lifting the Webb Ellis trophy than the French captain, who was competing in his fourth World Cup. 'One of us was

going to retire straight after this game,' said Wood, 'and we both knew it. I would love to play on but my shoulder is an accident waiting to happen and it's better to go out like this, however disappointing the result, than as the result of yet another injury.'

So Irish rugby bade farewell to one of its outstanding players and leaders, and the squad headed home to a diet of Celtic League and Heineken Cup fixtures and the 2004 Six Nations Championship. Eddie O'Sullivan, who had his contract extended for a further four years to take him past the 2007 World Cup, knew that he had some way still to go before Ireland could consider themselves worthy of a place among world rugby's elite.

David Humphreys (IRE) – 60th cap v France.

What they said...

Ireland coach Eddie O'Sullivan addresses his troops post-match.

Ireland: Keith Wood (captain)

"I don't have the temperament. Our coach Eddie O'Sullivan is cranky, but not as cranky as me. I would love to have stayed for another couple of weeks with this Irish team, but we lost to a fine French side."

The veteran hooker reflects on the game and explains that he will not be going into coaching.

France: Bernard Laporte (coach)

"I had to congratulate him personally for all he has done for rugby."

The France coach pays tribute to Keith Wood on the announcement of his retirement.

France: Fabien Galthie (captain)

"It was almost perfect. It was especially gratifying to go through the moves that we work on in training and to see so many of them come off."

The France captain is rightly delighted with the dominance that swept his side home against Ireland.

France: Bernard Laporte (coach)

"I don't care who the opposition is. We have the means to win this World Cup."

Coach Laporte sticks his neck out.

France captain Fabien Galthie in action v Ireland.

Business Goals

Partnership in Reliability

SKF and Wyko offering a comprehensive business solution

Partnership in Reliability is a unique partnership from SKF and Wyko. Through SKF Reliability Systems and Wyko Industrial Services, we are now able to provide a single integrated source for your business and productivity solutions. Our goal is to help our customers reduce total machine, procurement and inventory related costs to enhance productivity and strengthen profitability.

- Consultation
- Recommendation
- Training
- Implementation
- Review and Measurement
- On-going support

For more information on our integrated solutions please call the SKF marketing department: 01582 490049 or e-mail: marketing.uk@skf.com *or* please call Wyko Industrial Services marketing department: 0121 508 6341 or e-mail: marketing@wyko.co.uk

Strategic Drivers

Asset Efficiency

Plant Efficiency

Admin Efficiency

 SKF Distributor

Wyko Industrial Services

...much more than you imagine

QUARTER-FINAL
England v Wales

MICK CLEARY

Pass the smelling salts. Upstairs and downstairs a nation of England followers, whatever their ilk or status, spent this entire quarter-final in a state of high anxiety. The fat lady didn't mount the rostrum until the whistle was on its way to the mouth of referee Alain Rolland. Sure, England had clear water between them and the Welsh by then, but such was the daring brilliance of Wales's play, such was their unquenchable desire to reach out and experience places that other sides rarely visit, such was their urge to give it a lash and devil take the hindmost, that no Englishman could feel safe.

By the end, Welsh rugby had re-asserted itself in the consciousness of the sporting public and England had done the best thing they could do to shake themselves free of the pressure of being World Cup favourites by playing like complete also-rans. It was a match that altered the delicate balance of power – not that such calculations mean too much until the final reckoning is done. If sport were a precise science then Wales would probably not have bothered to turn up. They had lost 13 of their past 15 encounters with England, conceding an average scoreline in excess of 40 points. Their front-line side had also been roundly

BELOW **The one that got away. Wales lock Robert Sidoli loses control of the ball with the line at his mercy as he is tackled by England flanker Lewis Moody.**

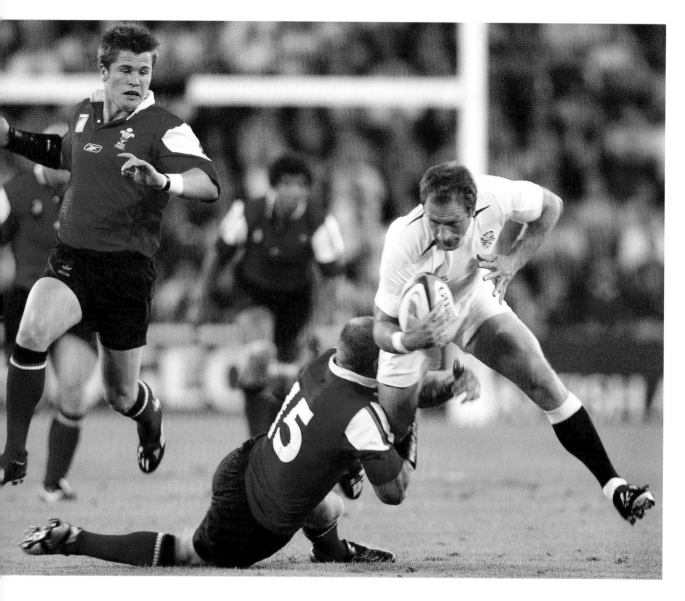

ABOVE **Supersub Mike Catt can't get away this time as he hauled down by Wales full back Gareth Thomas.**
FACING PAGE **Wing Dan Luger is the victim of a wicked bounce as his opposite number, live wire Shane Williams, closes in fast.**

beaten by England's second string in Cardiff in the first of England's three warm-up games. The portents were not good.

Mercifully sport is a game of harsh realities not scientific formulae. Wales played a game of heart and soul, not one of cold assessment. There was, of course, a lot of thought and careful planning in their approach; one that was superbly orchestrated by coach Steve Hansen. But it was the sheer vibrant, nerveless attitude of Wales that really struck home.

Never mind the land of their fathers being proud of them. The whole of planet rugby felt a warm afterglow after this swashbuckling match. Wales brought colour and verve, wild fancy and unbreakable spirit to the occasion. They brought twinkling feet and flickering hands as well, scoring three tries to England's one.

The Grand Slam champions were beaten senseless for long stretches of the first half by the Six Nations wooden spoonists. The transformation in fortunes was scarcely credible. The Welsh union may be fighting for financial survival. Its rugby team, however, once again looks to be a going concern.

It was a game to treasure, won through England's concerted drive and cussedness and, inevitably, the boot of Jonny

ABOVE **Fly half Stephen Jones touches down for Wales to finish off a counterattack worthy of the great Welsh sides.**
RIGHT **Fortune favours the brave. Colin Charvis scores from a line out following a penalty, having spurned the three-point option. Charvis had done exactly the same against New Zealand a week earlier.**

Wilkinson. As Wales chased, so they infringed. Wilkinson took due retribution with six penalties, five of them in the second half. He also picked a ball off his toes in the final second to drop a 40-metre goal. The edgy, haunted first-half figure finished with a flourish. His first kick of the evening struck a post; his last hit the mark. The romantics may talk a good game; the pragmatists invariably have the last word.

One of the few good England calls of the evening was to bring on Mike Catt at half-time. The Bath old stager stayed true to his roots, playing what was in front of him and not what was programmed into his head. What instructions had he been given at the interval with England on the rack, trailing 10-3? 'Nothing really,' said Catt, a late selection for the original squad after Alex King pulled out with injury. 'I was just told to go out and play my game. It was a question of going back to basics. We had to cut out our mistakes and just get on with it. I thoroughly enjoyed myself out there. It was an advantage to have been able to watch the first half from the touch line and see what needed to be done. Remember, too, that I've not had the six months of build-up pressure that the other guys have had to cope with.'

Catt gave England much-needed craft and sharpness in midfield, also claiming valuable tracts of territory with his kicking from hand. He had recovered from a stiff neck in midweek. Wales caused several of his colleagues a similar ailment.

Wales won the heart of every neutral – not that many were to be found among the raucous tribes of Suncorp Stadium. Those watching round the world, though, will have sided with the unfancied Welsh. Unfortunately the sympathy vote counts for nothing. Wales headed home, while England packed their bags for Sydney and a final fortnight of testing competition. It was the underdog that was left howling at the full moon.

England were far from at their best. At times they were a complete shambles, lacking composure and self-assurance. They look pinched and stilted. Their first-half display saw them bunched time and again in a narrow-side channel, forcing passes under pressure and making little headway. There was no patience or thrust to their game in those periods. 'We were guilty of playing in too narrow a space,' said England head coach Clive Woodward. 'We consciously put in more bodies there in an effort to contest the breakdown more effectively. We had been giving away too many penalties there. That aspect of our game was a lot, lot better with the penalty count 17-9 in our favour. Those that criticise us for not scoring tries should consider Wales's penalty [count]. Teams concede penalties when they are under pressure. But we did play in too tight a part of the field.'

There was a catalogue of disturbing errors. Going walkabout is a cherished part of Aboriginal culture – the practice may have a couple of new recruits. Dan Luger, a late call-up after the double withdrawals of Josh Lewsey and Iain Balshaw, was jittery and off-key. He dropped balls and hit a horrendous sliced clearance just before the interval. It was no surprise when his place was taken by Catt in the second half.

Ben Cohen will also look back in horror at the video nasty of his cross-kick from a tap penalty under the Welsh posts in the

25th minute. England were guaranteed three points from that position, yet Cohen grabbed the ball and punted left. Small problem – out there was the titch of the England team, Neil Back, up against the strapping Llanelli wing, Mark Jones. 'No, I wouldn't have made that decision if I'd been on the pitch,' said Clive Woodward. 'Ben wasn't thinking too cleverly.'

Nor were many others. Mike Tindall's angled kick in the 35th minute pitted lock Ben Kay up against wispy Welsh wing Shane Williams. It was no contest. From just inside his own 22, Williams backed himself. Quite right too. He made serious ground, scrum half Gareth Cooper took it on and found Gareth Thomas in support. From there, Williams got in on the act again, juggling the ball before flicking infield to Stephen Jones, who touched down. It was a try that evoked memories of some of the great scores from yesteryear. In times to come, different names will be recalled round firesides.

In that first half of English torment, the line out was shaky and the decision-making flawed. Even though England had more possession, they were profligate in turning over ball. They came out with fresh kit in the second half. They ought to have been wearing sackcloth and ashes.

Wales played smart rugby. They had worked out England from long ago but had kept their thoughts to themselves. Coach Steve Hansen knew that he had to put width on the ball and stretch England's defence, which tends to cluster in midfield. It worked a treat. Hansen had the personnel to make it happen, too, from the short but snappy Shane Williams to the tireless support workers in the pack, flanker Dafydd Jones and lock Robert Sidoli.

Wales returned home with their stock greatly enhanced after unsettling the two top-ranked teams, New Zealand and England, in successive weekends. 'Right now, there is no consolation in the thought that we've run them both close,' said Wales coach Steve Hansen. 'When you get as close as we have, it's gut-wrenching to lose. But the team has done themselves and their country proud. I hope we've put a smile on the face of Welsh rugby and got people excited. People have got to get behind all the changes made in Wales and become one nation again rather than a lot of villages. If this tournament has managed to do that, then it's been a success for us.'

How Wales ran. How they saw the gaps. How they took the game to England, not giving a tinker's cuss for reputation or percentage return. England were forced to scramble in defence

LEFT Wales looked highly dangerous with ball in hand. Here replacement scrum half Dwayne Peel leaves Jonny Wilkinson floundering as he runs at England.

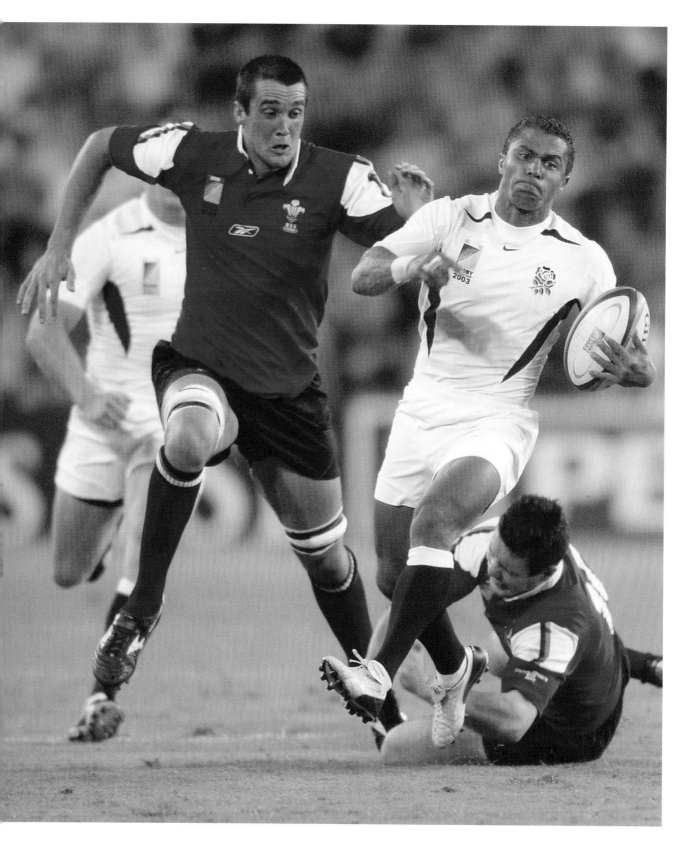

as Wales targeted their big men in the middle and ran round them. They made clever use, too, of the slither kick in behind, turning England and then harrying them.

It was a downfield hoof from Cooper that led to Wales's second try in the 35th minute. Cohen made the initial retrieve deep in his 22 but was then judged to have hung on to the ball. Wales kicked for touch rather than for the posts and were rewarded when Colin Charvis was driven over. Two tries in four minutes, and England were reeling.

It was 10-3 at the interval. But as England's cast list changed with the arrival of Catt so did their fortunes. They were back on level terms within three minutes following a sensational 60-metre break from Jason Robinson, who had received the ball deep in his half after Cohen had fielded a clearance kick from Cooper. Wales had shackled Robinson well all evening; not this time. Robinson sliced through three attempted tackles and zipped outside two other defenders. The final pass to Will Greenwood was measured and the latter dived in at the corner for his 30th England try.

FACING PAGE **They call him 'Billy Whizz'. Jason Robinson's searing acceleration leaves successive Welshmen for dead as he rockets out of defence to set up England's try.**
BELOW **Will Greenwood is on hand to finish off Robinson's work.**

Then Catt got to work, so too Wilkinson. Wales became reckless and ill disciplined. They gave away 17 penalties, a heinous figure when Old Dead-Eye is in opposition. By the 65th minute Wilkinson had put clear water between England and Wales with five successive kicks.

England ought to have closed out the game at that point. But where once they were mentally tough and settled, now they seem prone to feverish lapses. Hooker Steve Thompson conceded a daft penalty, allowing Wales to kick downfield. From the line out they attacked one way, then when the ball was brought back Ceri Sweeney's kick high and left saw Lawrence Dallaglio clamber back alongside Shane Williams. The ball ricocheted, enabling Martyn Williams to touch down. Wales were back at the races, but they couldn't quite hit the jackpot. Iestyn Harris scuffed a kickable penalty six minutes from time; Wilkinson was, by now, in his element. Fortune had favoured the hang-dogged.

England coach Clive Woodward was in bristling mood afterwards, cranky that his team had played so poorly, and abrasively defiant that it could all be put to rights. He was charmless and unnecessarily dismissive in the after-match press conference, verbally swatting away questions from French journalists. 'France are the stand-out team now aren't they?' said the England head coach in a tetchy exchange with French

journalists from *L'Equipe*. 'They must be favourites to win it – but they haven't played England yet. We've won again without playing anywhere near our best. I believe we'll beat France because we've got the talent and leadership to do so. We're winning through sheer bloody-mindedness. If we can get nous into our game then we'll be okay. If we play against France like we did tonight, then we've got no chance. We made some fundamental errors. France know us well. They know what sort of team is coming at them.'

Woodward later realised that he had been cranky and insensitive. He was also quick to defend Jonny Wilkinson after the fly half once more looked out of sorts. Where most people saw a crabbed, hesitant figure, one that visibly grew only when Catt appeared to take the pressure off him, the England head coach saw only confirmation of Wilkinson's unique standing in the world game. 'I thought Jonny was awesome at the weekend,' said

RIGHT **Colin Charvis comes to terms with defeat as Wales go down despite outscoring England by three tries to one.**
BELOW **This attempted dropped goal sailed wide, but Jonny Wilkinson succeeded with eight kicks to pull England through.**

Woodward. 'I've got no issue with him whatsoever. He'll start against France and I have no doubt that he'll have a major influence. You've got to remember that Jonny is a completely different No. 10 to anyone else playing the game, be it Michalak or Larkham or Spencer. That's not to say that he's necessarily better, just different. He's so aggressive, so much wants to get involved. You need to see the defensive work that he does, the number of rucks that he hits. He had to do that on Sunday at contact because that's the area we've been struggling at. He plays like a wing forward so you do need someone to step into the No.10 role to cover. But I don't want to change the way that Jonny Wilkinson operates. He's been like that since I've known him. That's him and he's a brilliant guy to work with. Why would you want to change him? The team have got to adapt to him.' That was the challenge facing England as they headed to Sydney.

Dafydd Jones – tireless for Wales.

What they said...

England: Clive Woodward (coach)

"We have not been thinking too cleverly. But we have won by sheer bloody-mindedness and nous.... If we play like we have at our worst we will lose to France, but at our best we will win. Against Wales in the quarter-final our defence was disappointingly weak. There was some strong language used at half-time when we were losing. But we are happy to stay in the tournament, even though we are way below our peak."

Steve Hansen – Wales coach.

Wales: Steve Hansen (coach)

"We scored four against New Zealand and three against England, who are supposed to have the unbreakable defence. We believe that we have done the nation proud, despite the defeats, and that we have put a smile back on the face of Welsh rugby."

Coach Hansen is proud of his side's try-scoring exploits.

Wales: Colin Charvis (captain)

"A lot of these 2003 World Cup players will be around for a long time in what must be a brighter future for us after our bad start to this important year."

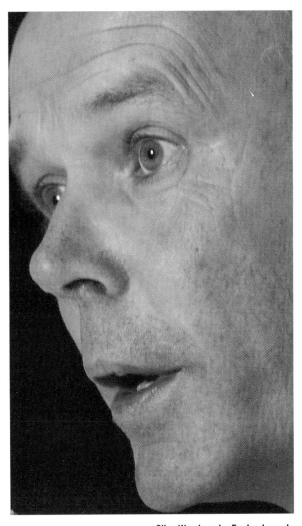

Clive Woodward – England coach.

NEW ZEALAND

Legend

AUSTRALIA

Legend

WALES

Legend

Never underestimate the importance of local knowledge.

What number is your "all time great"? When you're a local it's obvious.

At HSBC, we have banks in more countries than anyone else. And each one is staffed by local people.

We have offices in 79 countries and territories; Europe, Asia-Pacific, the Americas, the Middle East, and Africa.

Being local enables them to offer insights into financial opportunities and create service initiatives that would never occur to an outsider.

It means our customers get the kind of local knowledge and personal service that you'd expect of a local bank.

And a level of global knowledge and widely sourced expertise that you wouldn't.

HSBC ◀▶

The world's local bank

Issued by HSBC Holdings plc.

SEMI-FINAL
New Zealand v Australia

STEPHEN JONES

Australian rugby has enjoyed a magnificent run of success over the past 15 or 20 years. In 1999 Australia became the first country to win the World Cup twice, they defeated the British Lions in 2001 and the sport of rugby union has been boosted up in the country to such an extent that it has overhauled rugby league in terms of spectator interest and participation, even though at one stage league was light years ahead in both these areas. But even in their two winning finals, it is difficult to believe that Australia ever played so well as they did when comprehensively dumping New Zealand in the 2003 semi-final, in a glorious match in front of a capacity crowd at Telstra Stadium in Sydney.

It would be wrong to suggest that this wonderful occasion was the match that set Rugby World Cup 2003 alight, because in truth the tournament had been magnificent from the very start. But it was certainly a memorable occasion and one which finally united the whole of Australia behind the Wallabies.

It was not as if Australia had ever looked like losing any of their pool games, and they were only really taken to the wire in their final group match, against Ireland. But there were many observers, professional and otherwise, who suggested that this Australian team was well below par and that the host-country challenge would soon peter out.

PREVIOUS PAGE **Stirling Mortlock picks off Carlos Spencer's floated pass and sets off upfield to score Australia's try, leaving behind an incredulous Spencer and Justin Marshall.**
BELOW **Just beforehand, Lote Tuqiri pulled off this try-saving tackle to deny Mils Muliaina. Muliaina's attempt at the corner was referred to the TV official, who ruled that the full back had knocked on.**

Indeed, New Zealand were as high as 13-point favourites with many local and international bookmakers before the match, a rating which was based largely on the apparent brilliance of their high-scoring backs. Wiser heads preferred to have faith in the momentous motivational properties of a team hosting its own World Cup, and a few voices were also raised to point out that New Zealand's forward play was not quite from the top bracket.

Let us say that those who doubted New Zealand were borne out in spades. Australia began with a brilliant opening passage of play, they kept up an absolutely ferocious passion and intensity, they were never, never going to lose the match, and in all justice they would not have been flattered had the final margin been 25 points or more. In the stadium itself, and at all those areas dotted around Sydney where followers watched the action on giant screens, the joy was unconfined.

Australia were magnificent at retaining the ball, and huge credit must go to Eddie Jones and his coaches for the way in which, systematically, they sent out Australia equipped to take

New Zealand apart. The Australian scrum, not particularly highly rated in global terms, was resoundingly on top. The Australian line out, with Justin Harrison, Nathan Sharpe and replacement David Giffin particularly prominent, ruled the roost. Furthermore the Australian experiment of playing two open-side flankers in Phil Waugh and George Smith paid off because there was a relentless Australian energy at the breakdown and in the tackles. It was stirring, sustained and it almost stupefied the All Blacks.

But critics of the rather stodgy Australian team of 1999 were fascinated to see that the 2003 model had grafted on individuals of talent. Stirling Mortlock in the centre, Mat Rogers at full back and Lote Tuqiri on the wing were outstanding, running with passion and penetration and adding splashes of vivid colour to what was once a rather black-and-white unit.

On the other hand, New Zealand's supporters must have been thunderstruck. John Mitchell, the All Black coach, had done his best to produce bricks without straw. The way the domestic game in New Zealand is set up does tend to militate against the

production of genuine forwards of world class, with the country seemingly in thrall to faster, lighter and less formidable forwards. Goodness only knows what powerful giants such as Colin Meads, Sean Fitzpatrick and Olo Brown would make of it, but more than a few global observers believed that New Zealand were betraying a magnificent heritage of forward excellence to try to chase some abstract concept of entertainment.

It all seemed to work during the rather disappointing 2003 Tri-Nations competition, which New Zealand dominated. It also seemed to work during New Zealand's pool matches in this World Cup, because the likes of Italy, Wales, Tonga and even the pathetically feeble South Africans lacked the courage or the power to ask questions of the New Zealand pack.

Australia had no such problems. Some of the possession statistics of this semi-final were remarkable, with the forlorn New Zealand pack being dominated for possession. Before this match, the hit men, such as Joe Rokocoko, Doug Howlett and Carlos Spencer, were cruising around the field and eating up defences. But suddenly they were no longer on the front foot; and harassed by the Wallabies at every turn, it seemed that the fires of battle quickly died in them as what was at one stage superhuman was quickly reduced to the ranks of the mediocre.

Australia began as if determined not to kick the ball long to prevent the highly rated New Zealand back three from hitting them on the counterattack. Possibly Australia took this policy too far, because there were occasions when Steve Larkham and company would have done better to drill long kicks downfield behind the All Black wings. However, there is a line about the proof of the pudding, and it was the All Blacks who were eaten.

There was some thrilling rugby in the opening stages, because although Australia's dominance was obvious from the start, there was some defending to do early on, and both Wendell Sailor and Tuqiri were forced to make outstanding tackles in the Wallaby corners. It is just possible that those tackles prevented New Zealand from drumming up an irresistible momentum.

Certainly the All Blacks did no such thing. Carlos Spencer has always been a controversial figure in New Zealand rugby, with supporters claiming that he can break open a match at any time, but with his detractors claiming that he can often break open the match in favour of the opposition. That is precisely what he did on this occasion, floating a dangerous pass across the face of the Australian midfield, which Mortlock picked off to run 70 thrilling yards to score.

Australia continued to dominate and it was only desperate and often illegal defending by New Zealand which kept the score down. The immaculate Elton Flatley kept the pot boiling before

ABOVE **Skipper Reuben Thorne dives for the line and a New Zealand score after a glimpse of vintage Carlos Spencer opened up the Wallaby defence.**

half-time by kicking the conversion and two penalties, and as the match approached the interval, there was the obvious hope that Australia would go in 13-0 ahead. A blunder by Larkham soon changed all that, and at the time it seemed that he had put the match back into the balance. Larkham really should have been looking to nurse his team carefully into the half-time break with the 13-0 lead intact, but he tried to run the ball deep inside his own territory, after shaping to kick clear. He coughed up the ball, Spencer went on his way with it, and Reuben Thorne, otherwise miserably disappointing as the New Zealand captain, scored a try. The conversion by Leon MacDonald made it 13-7 at half-time.

The whole world expected a tumultuous New Zealand effort at the start of the second half, though some observers had noted that they simply had neither the power nor the ability to mount such an effort. With Larkham and Mortlock continuing to be inspirational, and with Australia running with the ball in hand, it was the home team who re-established themselves quickest. And they began to make the scores that they so deserved. Flatley may be nobody's idea of a new David Campese, but his sheer dependability as a footballing inside centre must be priceless for his coaches. Flatley kicked two more penalties to take it away to 19-7, with the only New Zealand reply a penalty from MacDonald.

New Zealand did have a few platforms of pressure in the second half, but by this time Spencer had become an alarmingly peripheral figure, often standing out wide as a fifth or sixth receiver when as the fulcrum of the team, he really should have been in there taking responsibility. MacDonald's penalty did make it 19-10 , but, perhaps amazingly for such a vaunted attacking combination, New Zealand never appeared on the point of scoring a try.

Indeed, their performance collapsed into indiscipline. Another dreadful illegal tackle by the controversial Jerry Collins, the Kiwi No. 8, knocked senseless the giant Sharpe. Furthermore players such as Collins, Richie McCaw and even MacDonald were very fortunate not to be sent to the sin-bin by English referee Chris White after their infringements became persistent. The only thing that could be said in their favour was that the sheer frustration they had to endure might have turned any man to sporting crime.

There was another largely token period of New Zealand pressure just after the hour mark, but an enormous kick by

Rogers brought some relief so that there was still a 12-point difference with only 11 minutes remaining. At around this stage, New Zealand coach Mitchell desperately tried to rotate his staff, in particular bringing off the inadequate David Hewett, the loose-head prop, and replacing him with Kees Meeuws. But even this move backfired, because Meeuws soon departed the field in a sorry state with a recurrence of a long-standing calf injury.

Although Flatley spoiled his immaculate record by missing a kick after yet another infringement by Collins, he did add a further penalty to give Australia breathing space and to cue in

BELOW **No. 8 Jerry Collins executes a high tackle on Wallaby Nathan Sharpe. The All Black escaped sanction, there being a suggestion that Sharpe was not at full height when Collins hit him.**

celebrations all over the city and all over the country. The Australians performed a lap of honour around the stadium after the match, an act which was criticised later by some of their own observers. Neutrals preferred to point out that when you have given one of the performances of your life in front of your own fans, then some communion with the people who have paid good money is richly appropriate.

Obviously, the result went down disastrously in New Zealand. It is often said, with the figures to prove it, that rugby disasters cost the New Zealand exchequer a fortune in lost production, and cause the whole country to slump in the shoulder region. Be that as it may, followers of New Zealand's grand rugby traditions would no doubt have been hoping at the end that yet another World Cup failure would knock technical and tactical heads

together and produce a New Zealand domestic game which, while still based partly on the concept of entertainment, would place more emphasis on forward play and quality possession. The fact is that while this was a stupendous Australian performance, it also laid bare that New Zealand, amazingly for a country with such rugby nous, has been trying for too long to ignore rugby realities, especially the realities of going forward, the realities of physical confrontation, and the reality that the match begins as a struggle for possession. Bricks without straw.

There was further good news for Australians afterwards. During the game Ben Darwin, the Wallaby prop, was taken from the field on a motorised stretcher after a scrum collapsed. At first he appeared immobile, but later he regained feeling and movement and the initial prognosis was good. 'I heard a crack and immediately called out "neck, neck, neck", and to his credit Kees Meeuws stopped pushing. This was fortunate because I'd lost feeling in my body and he could really have rushed me into the ground,' Darwin said later.

'While I was on the ground, I had no feeling from my neck down for about two minutes. It was terrifying, but the medical staff did a great job of getting me into the right position, and when I felt pins and needles in my arms and legs, it was a great relief.' It seemed in the aftermath of the game that Darwin might require some surgery, but fears of lasting damage were allayed.

ABOVE **We're through! Celebrations begin for Australia, while for the much-fancied All Blacks it's another semi-final exit.**
FACING PAGE **Australia's Mr Reliable, Elton Flatley, nails All Black runner Joe Rokocoko.**
FOLLOWING PAGE **It says it all. Mat Rogers reflects the feelings of a nation at the final whistle at Telstra Stadium.**

Australia motored on into the final. One of the truths of this tournament was that every team needed a ferocious workout before they could really reach their best. In the final analysis, Australia had been more strongly tested in the pool games. New Zealand, by contrast, had played several teams who fielded reserve players, preferring to preserve their first string for winnable matches. In this regard it may have been unfortunate for New Zealand that their quarter-final against South Africa, which was meant to be a titanic confrontation, petered out alarmingly in the face of feeble Springbok resistance.

Yes, New Zealand were the darlings of many. Yes, when their backs were given space they could be quick and deadly. But this Australian victory was a comeuppance. It was an introduction to reality, and it indicated, by putting a premium on forward power, that rugby has its balance correct between piano players and piano shifters. And what is any World Cup without a stunning effort from the hosts? Advance Australia, to the final.

2003

Justin Harrison (AUS) – towering presence.

What they said...

New Zealand: John Mitchell (coach)

We are not chokers. We were beaten by the better team. I cannot speak for previous New Zealand defeats at late stages of the World Cup. Australia won the hard inches. People will ask: 'Where was the traditional All Blacks' brain, skill and resilience? Certainly we lacked skilful execution at the important tackle area and some decisions were wrong. But we did our best to come back. There was a lot of slow ball or even no ball and that puts stress on the half backs. But I still believe in the All Blacks' way, and I am not resigning. I love coaching and my future is for my employers to decide. Nevertheless, I am accountable and I feel sorry for all New Zealanders.

New Zealand: Reuben Thorne (captain)

It will be tough for the public back home, but it's twice as tough for us to bear. We have come so far only to be heartbroken.

Reuben Thorne (NZL) and George Gregan (AUS).

Stirling Mortlock (AUS) takes his chance.

Australia: Stirling Mortlock (centre)

I was out of a team that was winning, but got my opportunity in the quarters. That try came when I was intending only to make a tackle. Then I found their pass coming into my hands and I kept on running for my first interception try.

Try scorer Stirling Mortlock covered 70-odd yards for his touchdown but had come from much farther away career-wise to have his chance.

Australia: Eddie Jones (coach)

We played reasonable football in patches and that was enough to win. But we still didn't attack with the necessary precision. We need to improve in line out and scrum to take control of a final. We are a better side when we attack and we kept kicking to a minimum because we are a team that thrives with the ball in hand. The praise should go to the forwards. They delivered the ball.

Coach Jones downplays his side's dominance.

Australia: George Gregan (captain)

That display was up there with the best I have been involved in. But credit must go to New Zealand for their play during this long year. They have taught us so much and we showed that we have taken on board the lessons they gave us.

WELL WORTH ANOTHER LOOK.

DISCOVERY

THE LAND ROVER EXPERIENCE

3 UNLIMITED MILEAGE WARRANTY The official fuel consumption figures in mpg (l/100km) for the vehicle shown are: Urban 22.2 (12.7), Extra Urban 31.4 (9.0) and Combined 27.4 (10.3). The official CO₂ emission is 284 g/km.

SEMI-FINAL
France v England

MICK CLEARY

t may not have been pretty, it may not have been spectacular, but it was convincing. With each swing of that Jonny Wilkinson boot – left foot, right foot, you name it, he can pot with it – French heads dropped still further. By the time the last of Jonny Boy's eight successful kicks went between the sticks at a rain-lashed Telstra Stadium, the England fly half might have been sending the ball into the French solar plexus, for they were down on their knees gasping for mercy at the feet of Mr Relentless.

ABOVE **The indefatigable Neil Back leaves Imanol Harinordoquy flat out as he takes off upfield. The England back row more than matched their French counterparts, despite pre-match hype.**
PREVIOUS PAGE **England scrum half Matt Dawson hangs on to a high ball in nightmare handling conditions at Telstra Stadium.**

Twenty-four points, five penalties and three dropped goals – game, set and match to England, 24-7. The fat lady is always on full alert when Wilkinson is in the mood, knowing that she might have to make an early appearance. So it proved.

England did as England do to win this game. If the semi-final the previous day had been a theatrical, energy-busting, unflagging, unexpectedly gripping contest with its unheralded outcome, then this match followed a far more predictable pattern. Or it did if you had followed proper form rather than taken a punt on the few impressive games that France had strung together so far in the World Cup. You had to admit that France had looked the part in those early pool romps as they racked up a stack of points against Fiji, USA, Japan, Scotland, and then, seemingly most tellingly, against Ireland in the quarter-final. True pedigree, though, runs deeper than a four-week cycle. France had been out of sorts through the year, unsure of their side and unsure of themselves. Players were left at home for the beleaguered summer trip to Argentina and New Zealand. Even so, France ought to have made a better fist of the tour.

England's foundations were built on altogether more substantial footings. They had not lost a Test of any real significance in 18 months. Their only loss in that period had been against France in Marseilles, but that 17-16 defeat was incurred by a second-string England side as Clive Woodward looked to fine-tune the fringe players in his World Cup squad. England had conviction and assurance on their side and in their side.

A lot of flimflam pre-match analysis focused on the ageing nature of the England team with its geriatric ward of thirty-somethings – Martin Johnson, Lawrence Dallaglio, Neil Back, Mike Catt, Richard Hill, Jason Leonard and the like. None of those commentators bothered to check the detail of England's double-whammy June victories over New Zealand and Australia, when the old stagers had been in their element. In Wellington and Melbourne it was the opposition that was blowing hard at the final whistle, not Johnson and his mates. England may well have stuttered by their own high standards during the World Cup, but they had faced down those difficulties and come through to win.

England showed character and resolve to win through to their second final, while France all but disintegrated as the Sydney heavens opened to rain on their World Cup parade. They had two men, wing Christophe Dominici and flanker Serge Betsen, sin-binned and were ragged, off-key and ill-disciplined in equal measure. They were lucky to finish with a full complement, with Betsen a serial offender. He was later cited for an alleged kick. It was an all too familiar scenario for France. How often have they been plagued down the years by their hot-headed blemishes?

England may well have made them look a shadow of their former selves, but France also need to look within. They had shown impressive form in the tournament, but when it came to the high-octane occasion they had no one to match the sangfroid of Jonny Wilkinson or the ferocious all-enveloping desire of Martin Johnson and his pack of forwards. Neil Back in particular gave tireless and intelligent support throughout, ensuring that England gained a decisive advantage at the breakdown. They didn't waste that ball. 'A lot was written beforehand about the power of the French back row,' said Clive Woodward afterwards. 'Our back row obliterated them.'

The contrast in fortunes between the teams was neatly captured just after the hour mark when a double substitution by France saw two of their key players, Betsen and fly half Frederic Michalak, trudge off the field. These were the men that were supposed to haunt and taunt England – the former by suffocating Wilkinson at source, the latter by dancing through the English defence at will. Neither happened. Betsen was yellow-carded for a late tackle on Wilkinson in the 53rd minute, while Michalak showed the nerves of anxious youth, fluffing kicks at goal and underclubbing several up-and-unders. 'I was rubbish,' admitted the 21-year-old later. And so he was.

Creative tension proved to be the more productive means of preparation for this semi-final than designer chic harmony. While France unwound during the week at laid-back Bondi Beach, England had a clear-the-air meeting behind closed doors at their Manly base and exposed a few home truths. The upshot was that England never appeared fazed or rattled when France went into

BELOW **Frederic Michalak aims a kick over the advancing England forwards. After barely putting a foot wrong in the tournament to date, the fly half could hardly do anything right against England.**

ABOVE **England wing Jason Robinson struggles in vain to hold back Serge Betsen. The France breakaway made it to the line and a try despite the last-ditch intervention of Richard Hill.**

an early lead; they worked their way back into contention by the time-honoured virtues of honest graft up front and well-marshalled play behind the scrum. France were too casual for their own good. When the squeeze came on, they were jittery and out of sorts. They dropped balls, sliced clearance kicks and never established any sort of foothold in England's territory.

The dreadful conditions made it difficult for either side to get a firm grip of things. There were errors on England's part, too, especially early on when their positional kicking was wayward. But once the radar got locked on, and once the forwards began to exert control, then it was France who found themselves continually on the back foot.

England are masters at managing the moment. They have battled through all sorts of testing circumstances in this tournament, finding solutions as they go along. Betsen's try in the tenth minute might have frayed the nerves of a lesser side, but England rode out that little squall to head into the half-time break with a five-point advantage at 12-7.

Referee Paddy O'Brien had to go to the TV match official, Andrew Cole, to confirm Betsen's score, the flanker having snaffled a ball at a line out and hared towards the try line. He was hauled down just short by Jason Robinson but slithered over on

the greasy surface. Richard Hill managed to get an arm underneath the French flanker, but Cole adjudged that Betsen had managed to get proper downward pressure.

Hill, playing his first game since England's opening match of the tournament against Georgia – one cut short for him by a hamstring problem that plagued him for four weeks – was caught napping when he failed to close the gap at the rear of the line out. Thereafter, though, Hill played a commanding role. It was no coincidence that his presence on the field led to the much-vaunted opposition half-back pairing having their quietest game of the World Cup. Hill, in his understated, unassuming way, has that sort of effect.

France failed to capitalise on that early advantage. England were fretful themselves in those early stages, but Michalak could not make it tell as he pushed two penalty kicks wide. The fault lines were already beginning to appear. Wing Christophe Dominici had a rush of blood in the 23rd minute when he flicked out his right leg as Jason Robinson cut inside. The England wing went crashing to the turf as if he had been felled by Norman 'Bites Your Legs' Hunter. Dominici hurt himself in the process and was substituted after his ten minutes in the sin-bin. His reckless rather than intentional challenge was symptomatic of France's jumpy display. 'We were very edgy and fragile when it mattered,' said French coach Bernard Laporte. 'The blame has to be at our own door. It's too easy to take refuge in the weather. It was the same for England. It was not them that knocked on several times and lost balls in their line out. They showed flexibility and we did not. The better team won, that is for sure.'

England took hold of the game and never let go. You might argue that the conditions played into their hands. You might peddle that line, but it doesn't cut much ice. England never looked in the slightest danger. France were dreadful, a woeful imitation of the team that had demolished Ireland in the quarter-final. In part, England made them look this way; in part, they choked, unable to cope with the pressure of the occasion. 'At the back of everyone's mind, this was the game that we had been waiting for,' said Clive Woodward. 'The Tuesday before, we had a meeting and there was a lot of bad-natured anger from the coaches and a lot of good-natured anger from the players when we saw the tape of that Wales game. We handled it all well.'

Mike Catt's recall to the front line eased some of the burden of responsibility on Wilkinson. Catt did not settle immediately, miscuing some kicks. He is a very different player to the man he replaced, Mike Tindall, and although he does not punch his way across the gain line in the same muscular manner that his Bath team-mate does, Catt's ability to keep defences turning with his kicking game is a crucial addition to England's repertoire.

Wilkinson seems more at ease with him alongside. The England fly half snapped over two dropped goals in the first half, making sure that his side took full advantage when they got within range. It was a similar story in the second half as he landed two penalties and a dropped goal. 'They tell me that Wilkinson is dead,' said Laporte. 'He didn't look dead to me. He played a great match. You saw the difference today with Freddie Michalak.'

Captain Fabien Galthie tried all he knew to right the ship but to little avail. 'It is not Freddie's fault,' said Galthie, who announced his retirement the next day. 'He is human not a machine. We all dreamt of a different end. It was not to be. Eh, *voilà*.'

Jason Leonard came on as a blood replacement for Phil Vickery in the fourth minute and became the most-capped player of all time, passing Philippe Sella's mark of 111 caps. He was on the field barely 60 seconds at this point, although he reappeared just before the end for Trevor Woodman.

And so every cobwebbed Pom-bashing cliché in the cupboard was dusted down in readiness for the re-enactment of the old Anglo-Aussie rivalry. 'It's the dream final,' said England head coach Woodward afterwards. 'We came here to win the ultimate prize and now we're one match away. We'll have to play the game of the tournament to beat Australia.'

Not even the foul weather that saturated the surface and made handling so difficult could dampen the enthusiasm of the 40,000 England supporters in the capacity crowd. They made Telstra Stadium seem like Twickenham. 'The fans were awesome, absolutely brilliant and I'm sure that there will be a lot of people in England now trying to book flights for the final,' said England captain Martin Johnson.

As Johnson and his team turned to salute the crowd at the final whistle there was a special cheer for Wilkinson, the butt of so

BELOW **Christophe Dominici has a brainstorm and trips Jason Robinson as he cuts inside. The France wing picked up a yellow card and an injury as a result.**

much criticism in the build-up. The boot is invariably mightier than the word, and Wilkinson showed his composure under pressure. His performance was in marked contrast to the rising star of the game, Frederic Michalak, who fell to earth in no uncertain fashion with four successive penalty misses. The young pretender may have had squatting rights on Wilkinson's throne, but he was well and truly evicted in this semi-final.

There could not have been a greater contrast in style from Saturday's semi-final between Australia and New Zealand, which was played in sultry temperatures. The thermometer dropped almost 20 degrees Celsius, with the leaden-sky backdrop more akin to a winter's evening in Scunthorpe than early summer in Sydney. French coach Laporte must have looked at the blackening skies in mid-afternoon and inwardly groaned. Clive Woodward, though, had little truck with the notion that the weather played into England's hands. 'The conditions were the conditions,' said Woodward matter-of-factly. 'I've been to France on holiday and it rains a lot there too. I was confident that we'd have beaten France on a dry, hard pitch too.'

Woodward did concede that if he hadn't already selected Mike Catt over Mike Tindall then he would have made the change prior to kick-off once he saw the storm clouds roll in. The England coach has been a lone voice in these parts in his belief right from day one that Australia would be the team to beat in this

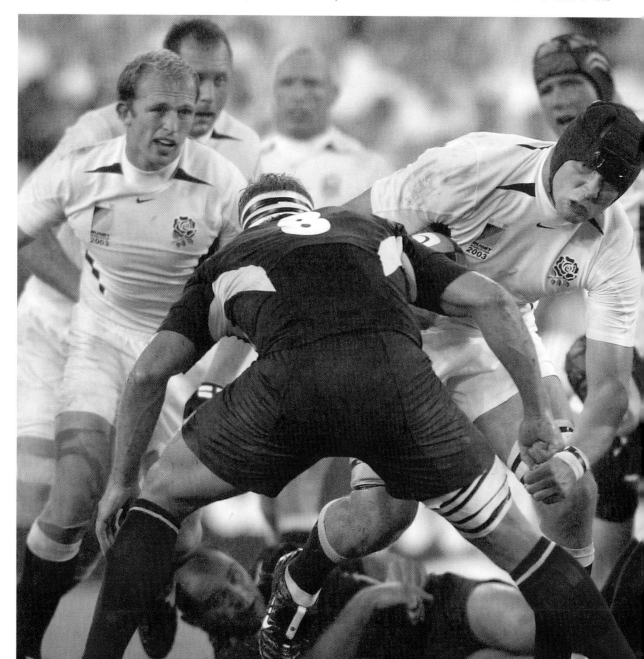

tournament. The Wallabies beat New Zealand 22-10 to go through to their third final. 'I'm delighted to be playing Australia, who are a real quality team,' said Woodward, whose team have beaten the Wallabies four times in succession. 'I admire them. Even though they've not always been at their best, they've got to the final through sheer force of character. I've been surprised how much stick they've had. They produced the best 40 minutes of the tournament in that first half against New Zealand. Our objective in coming here was to win the World Cup. I'd be very, very disappointed even now if we were to come second. As for the Pom-bashing, it's no more than banter. If you get upset by that then you shouldn't be in the job.'

It was only five months ago that England recorded their first ever victory over the Wallabies in Australia, beating the World Cup holders 25-14 in Melbourne. 'I don't think that result is too relevant now,' said Martin Johnson. 'They've raised the intensity of their game a few notches since than. They're a very clever, very shrewd side. They know how to peak and how to nullify an opponent, which they did in beating one of the tournament favourites on Saturday. When you get to this stage, the mental factor is as important as the physical one. You saw that with Australia as they ground down New Zealand. And we had to come through a bit of pressure after Betsen's try. But we kept going. If we've got to win ugly, then fine. I'd rather be playing on Saturday than having to come back for the third-fourth play-off on Thursday. We trained in the heat all week and then got a downpour. It's been a difficult week, but we dealt with it. I asked the guys to play their biggest game of the tournament and they did it. I wanted them to play with a lot of emotion and be physical to get the go-forward.'

The Wallabies had already retreated to their base at Coffs Harbour in coastal New South Wales by the time England kicked off in Sydney. 'England were very impressive,' said Wallaby coach Eddie Jones. 'They put enormous pressure on France and stopped them getting across the gain line. Wilkinson was excellent in the way that he controlled field position.'

The 24-year-old has been on the psychiatrist's couch over the past week as a succession of interrogators pondered his supposedly crumbling stability. The scrutiny didn't faze Wilkinson in the slightest. 'I've not had a clue about all the interest in my game,' said Wilkinson. 'Everyone's entitled to their opinion. I'm everyone's property when I represent my country. The only people I do want to try and please are the guys here next to me, Clive Woodward and Martin Johnson. It's been a satisfying evening, that's for sure. We handled some things very well today.'

Johnson was more than impressed. 'Someone asked in the week if Jonny had turned the corner. I couldn't believe the question. Jonny controlled things brilliantly. The stick that has been coming his way has been totally unwarranted. His kicks today kept us ticking over while Michalak's kicking under pressure wasn't that great and hurt their chances.'

This was a night for a mighty team effort. England did not disappoint on that count.

LEFT **Stand by to repel the enemy! Imanol Harinordoquy braces himself for the full impact of England lock Ben Kay.**
FOLLOWING PAGE **Jonny Wilkinson knocks over his final penalty of the evening, but the door had already slammed on France.**

Jason Leonard (ENG) – record 112 caps.

What they said...

France: Bernard Laporte (coach)

❝Our kicker is not a machine. He is a mere man. Jonny Wilkinson is alive and well and kicking like a machine. And the rain had a massive impact on the game. Perhaps we need to learn a kicking style in such conditions. We conceded too many penalties and had two players sin-binned. But that's the effect of Wilkinson's pressure. England were spectacularly good in the rain. They made far fewer mistakes.❞

Coach Laporte acknowledges two differences between France and England.

France: Fabien Galthie (captain)

❝It was a close match only for the first quarter. In the second half when we were playing against the wind it was always going to be England's game. It's rugby logic. We are not as heavy as England. But we should be able to play in sun and rain. I hope the final is a special, memorable event and if that is the case the result is not relevant to me.❞

Martin Johnson (ENG) and Fabien Galthie (FRA) at no-side.

Coach Laporte and manager Jo Maso (right) look on the bright side.

England: Clive Woodward (coach)

❝The only word to use about my emotions tonight is 'proud'. I honestly believe that we could have beaten France in dry, hard conditions just as we did in the wet. It rains in France as well. They can't blame the weather.... After their try I was confident that they would not score another and when Jonny kept adding the three points it became increasingly difficult for them to play catch-up.❞

England: Martin Johnson (captain)

❝He [Wilkinson] controlled the game brilliantly. The criticism he took in midweek was unwarranted. He was at the heart of our 'ugly' win and if winning 'ugly' is the way into the final then fine by me.❞

England: Jonny Wilkinson (fly half)

❝Most games in this World Cup have been in the dry, but we have always trained and prepared for anything that the opposition, the referees or the weather throw at us. Clearly, it was not going to be a spectacle, so we went out to win by any means and the kicking chances fell for me.❞

England: Richard Hill (flanker)

❝I take responsibility for the try and I did my level best not to let it get me down and to make up for the missed tackle.❞

Instead of First Class and Business Class, Delta Air Lines offers you BusinessElite® – the business class appreciated by frequent fliers.

How do you describe a level of comfort that lets you step off an eight-hour transatlantic flight feeling more relaxed than when you boarded? Could it be the fact that Delta has removed all middle seats to offer you more space perhaps? Or the generous freedom of movement? Or the way your seat adjusts perfectly to your every wish?

In all probability, it's all these and more. Because for BusinessElite customers, comfort starts long before they even take their seats, thanks to a special Priority Check-In Service and the spacious Business Lounge. Not to mention the attentive service of our friendly flight attendants.

Then there's the in-flight cuisine. No, not catering, for this is a different class entirely. Savor an utterly delicious five course menu and you soon forget how high you are flying – or, for that matter, that you are on an aircraft at all. Our award-winning Vinum™ programme is the perfect accompaniment to your food.

And when, over brandy afterwards, you discover the laptop socket in your seat console, you probably won't even be surprised –– though we trust you'll appreciate it just as much as the personal phone, the large storage space, and the integrated lamp. To round it all off, Delta offers a truly comprehensive entertainment programme with a choice of six films, music and video games for the ultimate in à la carte relaxation.

In France, they say merci. In England, it's thanks, in Italy it's grazie. At Delta Air Lines, we say „150% bonus miles" – our own very special way of saying thank you for choosing to fly BusinessElite. For more information on Delta log on to www.delta.com or call reservations on 0800 414 767.

BUSINESS*elite*™
▲ Delta

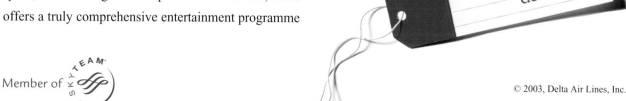

▲ Delta
delta.com

THIRD-PLACE PLAY-OFF
New Zealand v France

ALASTAIR HIGNELL

ABOVE **Reuben Thorne leads out New Zealand alongside Tony Marsh, who has the honour of taking the field first for France against the country of his birth for the third-place play-off at Sydney.**

This was a game that no one wanted to play in, but 62,111 people wanted to watch. Without a doubt, New Zealand wanted to win it more. Coach John Mitchell's job was on the line, and the memory of the failure in the 1999 third-place play-off in Wales was far too painful. The team then was publicly humiliated, the final straw being their arrival back in Auckland after a 13,000-mile flight to find that baggage handlers at the airport had daubed 'Losers' all over their suitcases. France briefly threatened to tear up the script – as they had done so thrillingly in the 1999 semi-final against the All Blacks – but in the end accepted a not too severe thrashing.

A third-place play-off match may make a lot of sense to marketers and broadcasters, but to players – especially players still reeling from the crushing disappointment of losing a World Cup semi-final only days before – it has next to no appeal. The respective managements made all the right noises – 'It is part of the tournament, we will have to deal with the situation,' said Mitchell, while French manager Jo Maso professed that his side

ABOVE **The heir to Galthie's crown? Dmitri Yachvili, whose brother Gregoire, a flanker, represented Georgia in the tournament, gets a pass away. The scrum half dropped a goal as well as kicking a penalty and a conversion in the match.**

were looking forward to taking on a disappointed New Zealand and were confident that the team spirit built up over the tournament would bring them the win they deserved. However, the players themselves were noticeably tight-lipped. Only All Black reserve hooker Mark Hammett broke silence with the terse comment that the match was 'pointless'.

New Zealand picked their strongest available side, with Steve Devine replacing Justin Marshall at scrum half in the only change from the line-up that had collapsed so unexpectedly against Australia in the semi-final. The team that only two days previously had been named as the IRB's international team of the year had some amends to make and maybe a coach's job to save. The label of 'chokers' – unwillingly picked up after an unexpected failure in the 1995 final against South Africa and heartbreakingly hung on to in that 1999 semi-final – will dog the All Blacks for some time to come. At least here was a chance to prove that they could not play as naively and ineffectively as they had done five days before.

The French players were not even afforded the opportunity. Coach Bernard Laporte made 13 changes from the side that had been swamped by England in a Sydney rainstorm the previous Sunday. Only prop Sylvain Marconnet and centre Tony Marsh – given the opportunity to line up against the land of his birth – were retained. Fabien Galthie, talismanic captain and veteran of four World Cups, had already announced his retirement and had in fact gone home for a family funeral. Dmitri Yachvili, for so long a frustrated understudy, was at last given the chance to show what he could do, as were exciting young backs Pepito Elhorga and Clement Poitrenaud and more seasoned forwards Patrick Tabacco and Sebastien Chabal.

No one, however, could shake off the lethargy brought on by a hot, muggy night. Everything about the opening exchanges seemed quaintly old-fashioned. The Marseillaise was sung at half-cock, the All Black haka was performed in an almost apologetic manner, and neither set of players displayed a fraction of the intensity they had shown in the semi-finals.

The All Blacks at least indicated that they had learnt some lessons from their defeat by Australia. Under pressure from the Wallabies, their back three speedsters – Doug Howlett, Mils Muliaina and Joe Rokocoko – were bottled up by some ferocious tackling, and New Zealand had demonstrated an inability to come up with a Plan B. Against a far less committed France, All Black fly half Carlos Spencer was relaxed enough to vary his game. Not only were the crowd treated to a series of outrageous, behind the back, 'blind' passes, they were also treated to his full repertoire of kicks from hand. One of his early specialities – the so-called banana kick off the outside of his right boot – almost produced a try down the left for Rokocoko. Other variations inevitably made ground and ensured constant panic in the French defence.

When Spencer has space in which to operate, as he was allowed in every match in the World Cup except for the crucial one against Australia, he can torment an opposition to distraction. With the French falling off him in this game, the outside half was able to fashion two sublime first-half tries. For the first, scored by Chris Jack, a clever flick from Spencer freed MacDonald down the left before a short pass from No. 8 Jerry Collins sent the giant lock galloping over the line. For the second, Spencer cleverly delayed a short pass to full back Mils Muliaina, whose pace and angle of run allowed him to break the first line of defence and whose equally clever inside pass to Howlett created an exhilarating try under the posts.

Both tries were converted – the first by MacDonald, the second by replacement Daniel Carter – while all the French could manage for their first-half efforts were a penalty goal and an almost apologetic dropped goal from Yachvili. The scrum half was also closest to scoring a try for Les Bleus when a series of close-quarter drives from the French led to the former Gloucester man being held up inches short of the All Black line.

The French, it seemed, were lucky to be still in the match at half-time. Although the statistics showed that they had enjoyed 50 per cent of the territory and 44 per cent of the possession, the figures also showed that France had had to make nearly twice as

BELOW **Lock Chris Jack eludes France left wing David Bory to round off a Carlos Spencer-inspired move and score the All Blacks' opening try of the evening.**

many tackles as the All Blacks. Something, it seemed, had to crack in the second period. Yet hopes of an upset were briefly kindled when, minutes after the resumption, France put together a series of attacks inside the All Blacks' 22: a long pass from Yachvili and a short feed from David Bory saw the lively Elhorga pick a great line and show great pace to cross under the posts.

Three All Black tries in less than ten minutes put paid to any such notions. The first had more than a touch of farce about it; the second more than a touch of controversy. The All Blacks had been in trouble after a superb run from replacement centre Brian Liebenberg, only for a half-charged-down clearance kick to bounce kindly for New Zealand's outstanding flanker Richie McCaw. A couple of swift passes later, and a desperately back-pedalling French defence had no chance of catching Rokocoko as he scored in the left corner.

Almost immediately, New Zealand scored again as Nicolas Brusque, another replacement in the French back line, fumbled a

harmless kick into touch and then turned his back on a sharply taken short line out by Howlett. To make matters worse for France, the referee, Chris White of England, failed to spot that Howlett's initial put-in to scrum half Steve Devine had not travelled the necessary five metres, and the wing was able to put Brad Thorn over for a try under the posts. Carter converted both these tries, as well as a third scored shortly afterwards by Muliaina, after the full back had been put clear by a long pass from centre Aaron Mauger.

At 35-13, the French were dead and buried, and everyone in the ground sat back and waited for the expected avalanche of

FACING PAGE **All eyes on the ball, as France full back Clement Poitrenaud challenges his opposite number, Mils Muliaina.**
BELOW **Doug Howlett, who scored New Zealand's second try and whose seven tournament scores put him at the top of the try-scoring table with fellow All Black Muliaina, with only the final to go.**

points. But the All Black forwards became obsessed with polishing up their close-quarter, pick-up-and-drive routines, while France, with Chabal to the fore, to a large extent held firm. Marty Holah, showing exceptional power in forcing his way over the line from ten metres, did score a further try, but by then the match, like the French players, was on its last legs. The final blast of Chris White's whistle was a merciful release for all on the pitch.

High up in the stands, New Zealand coach John Mitchell was obviously not so sure. For fully half an hour after the match ended, he sat with his coaching co-ordinator, Robbie Deans, staring out over the empty arena. Both men knew that, for all that the third place their team had just achieved was one better than in 1999, for all that they had coached the All Blacks to a glorious Tri-Nations title in 2003, for all that they had prised the Bledisloe Cup from Australia's grasp, and for all that their All Blacks had set the rugby world alight with the brilliance of their attacking game, they had failed where it mattered most – in a World Cup semi-final the previous week. That their team had just scored six tries in overwhelming France was no consolation at all.

If anything, it made a third-place play-off match seem even more meaningless, even more irrelevant. In the weeks leading up

to the match, there was talk of scrapping the fixture, or of replacing it with some sort of final for the developing nations. That is for the International Board to decide. Although they use the third-place play-off to help decide proceedings for the next World Cup, and although 62,000 people paid good money to watch it in Sydney, the board should, if only for the sake of the players, be actively considering an alternative.

FACING PAGE **All Black centre Aaron Mauger finds himself on the wrong end of a Sebastien Chabal special.**
RIGHT **Dreaming of what might have been? Or putting it all in perspective? Imanol Harinordoquy (clothed) and Frederic Michalak enjoy an after-match beer on the pitch at Telstra Stadium.**
BELOW **Would John Mitchell continue as All Blacks coach? He had achieved so much, yet the ultimate prize had eluded him.**

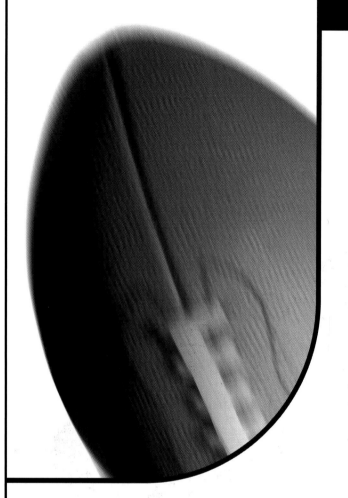

FINAL
Australia v England

JOHN INVERDALE

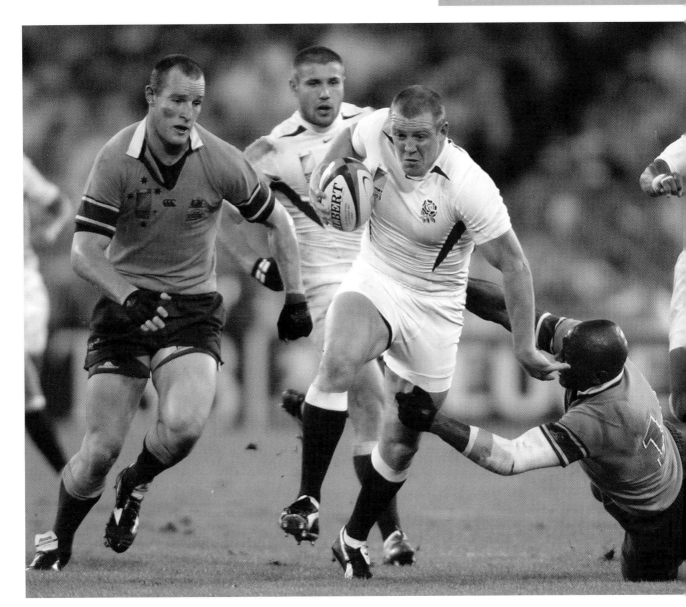

ABOVE **Wallaby right wing Wendell Sailor can't hold Mike Tindall as the England centre bursts through the Australian line. Tindall started ahead of Bath colleague Mike Catt and fully justified his inclusion.**

World Cup final day. One minute past midnight. It was pelting down, but nobody seemed to care. The lights of Darling Harbour sparkled in the rain, and all around the England fans talked of impending glory. Johnno and Jonny. They'd do it. Captain Fantastic and Superman. Any team with both of them in simply couldn't lose. When Andre Watson blew his whistle to start the match, it had barely stopped pouring down

in the intervening 20 hours. A bedraggled Sydney was reeling under a tidal wave of white replica shirts. The city was alive to the sound of rugby.

The details of what happened in the next couple of hours are almost immaterial. Let's face it. Had it not been for that Russian linesman in 1966, who'd remember anything of the game except Hurst's goal hitting the roof of the net and Kenneth Wolstenholme's immortal commentary: 'They think it's all over. It is now'?

Geoff Hurst wore the No. 10 jersey, and so did Jonny. He doesn't have a surname. Or indeed need one. He's Jonny. A bit like Martina or Boris or Tiger. Geoff is now Sir Geoff; Jonny is booked in at Buckingham Palace, when the Queen has a moment. For, with a further period of extra time beckoning, and the score locked at 17-all, England won a line out and launched an attack at the Australian line. You've seen the footage so often, you hardly need me to describe it. Johnno and Jonny. Martin Johnson drives into a ruck. The ball comes back, and Jonny, sitting in the pocket, swings his right boot. 'They think it's going over. It is. Now.' A ball over a crossbar, and a nation over the moon. That makes it some kick.

In a way that's all you need to know. It's what the sporting history books will recall. Of the five World Cup finals, only two have offered incidents to recount to grandchildren, and they're both dropped goals. Joel and Jonny. Anyway. Back to the story.

Australia scored first. The England line-up had Jason Robinson marking Lote Tuqiri, and the possible folly of that was underlined within five minutes as Stephen Larkham sent a massive cross-kick into the night sky. The giant former rugby league winger outjumped the not-so-giant former rugby league winger to score in the corner. Elton Flatley's conversion hit the post. How crucial was that to be!

Tuqiri, it should be said, had a good match. Mat Rogers, the second element of the Australian rugby league trio, took another step towards proving what a magnificent athlete he is – and union player he's about to become. It should have the been the ideal night for a man called Sailor, but Wendell had a stinker. The most high-profile convert of them all was found wanting on the biggest stage of all. He has a massive amount of rethinking to do if he's to ever be regarded as a successful acquisition by the Australian RFU.

So it was 5-0. Then Jonny had his first shot at goal. You don't need to watch where the ball goes when Jonny kicks it. You just

FACING PAGE **Lote Tuqiri beats Jason Robinson to Stephen Larkham's cross-field kick. He went on to convert his catch into a Wallaby try.** BELOW **England lock Ben Kay spills the ball forward with the Wallaby try line beckoning.**

watch him. If he picks up the kicking tee straightaway, it's over. If he watches the kick, it's not over. A fairly easy rule of thumb.

So 5-3 it was, but Australia were running the show as the rain came down. Yet England's defence was rock solid. This was, after all, a clash between the two best defences in the competition, so tries were going to be at a premium. The

Wallabies couldn't score another one for the next 95 minutes. England slowly but surely worked their way back into the game. Dawson darting; Dallaglio driving. Cohen was tackled off the ball by Larkham, and in a theatrical football-like gesture his World Cup winning Uncle George would have been proud of flung his arms to the heavens. Penalty. Jonny. Into the lead 6-5.

The England No. 10 had by this time flattened Flatley in a hit reminiscent of his tackle on Ntamack in Paris. He'd sent one touch-finder 65 metres downfield. He'd kicked two penalties. The haunted figure of earlier in the tournament had found a certain inner calm, you felt. If you're the best, you have to show it when it matters most.

He did miss a dropped-goal attempt, mind you. In fact he missed more than one. But when he got one late in the game...

Back to the first half. The England line out was pretty much a mess. Balls over the back to no one in particular but often fielded by a green-and-gold shirt. A slippery ball was no doubt to blame, but only partly. It was an area of their play that England were highly critical of afterwards. But they had the nudge in the scrum. Cohen bashed through a forlorn Sailor, who was shipwrecked on the right. Woodman was penalised at a set piece. Flatley missed. (If you don't kick your goals...)

It was all a bit hit-and-miss. A shocking kick from Larkham. A bad throw from Thompson. A great run from Tindall, who fully justified his selection ahead of Catt. And then the moment when England proved they could score a try. Not that they really needed to prove it, because three against the Wallabies in the summer had kind of made their case. But it was a classic.

Dallaglio breaking from a scrum fed his outside half bursting towards the 22, and his pass to Robinson speeding up on the left wing was brilliant. The Sale man touched down, and barked 'Come on!' to the cameras. No better time to score than just before half-time. 14-5 – the conversion astray from wide out. A nine-point margin at the break. England could have been out of sight, but Ben Kay dropped the ball with the line at his mercy. He didn't just drop the ball, he almost dropped the World Cup.

A tough call for the Wallabies now, but they did have the wind behind them. Despite that, it was England who began the stronger. Had Richard Hill not been penalised for obstruction, Ben Cohen might have barged his way through for a try. Rogers made a rare error of judgment from a mighty Tindall kick and let the ball bounce. England in the Aussie 22 again. A score now, and it was goodnight Matilda.

But the balance of power began inexorably to shift. England offside at a ruck. Flatley penalty. 14-8. Only one score in it. More line-out errors. The first game at Telstra Stadium all those weeks earlier between the Wallabies and the Pumas had been notable for one of the most inept displays of line-out play by the Argentinians. The tournament had come full circle.

And by now, boy was it raining. The game was in a lull. Too many stoppages and resets at the scrums. Andre Watson called the front rows together. 'Guys. There are millions watching this, and you're stuffing it up.' Phil Vickery handles on the ground. Flatley. 14-11.

LEFT 'Come on!' England's own rugby league convert Jason Robinson skids to a halt and a try, having beaten fellow ex-league player Mat Rogers to the Australian line.

2003

So tense and nervous heading to the final quarter, but very few try-scoring chances. The team that makes the fewest errors will win. Everyone knows. Jonny at this point is a bit-part player. The game's going on around him. The calm before...

Mortlock – so brilliant against the All Blacks – makes a scything run. Jonny returns to the fray and pulls him back by his shorts. That could have been the moment. Instead it's England who head downfield. Greenwood drops the ball, but England seem to have righted the ship. When Australia get into the England 22, why does Stephen Larkham not attempt a dropped goal? Remember the semi-final four years earlier? Is this some kind of doctrinal decision? We refuse to go down the Jonny line.

I make a note that we haven't had a single rendition of 'Swing Low' or 'Matilda' in the entire second half. 'Thank God', some might say. Tension indescribable. Noise overwhelming. Wallabies throwing everything at England. Mortlock again. Is this the winning score? Smack. Hit by you know who. He kicks goal. He throws try-scoring passes. He makes try-saving tackles.

England with one hand on the cup. A scrum goes down. Referee Andre Watson blows. Not a penalty? Not to the Wallabies? Why would England do that? They were in complete control of the scrummage.

Elton Flatley lined up the kick, ten metres in on the England 22. He knew that the biggest television audience ever for a rugby match was watching around the world. The biggest ever for a game of any description in Australia was watching. He knew that if he missed, Australia had lost. His heartbeat was probably audible in Alice Springs. He kicked it. And we had extra time. Didn't something similar happen in '66? Weren't England ahead, only to be hauled back at the last? This is spooky.

RIGHT **Nerves of steel. Elton Flatley's penalty for Australia on the stroke of no-side sends the 2003 World Cup final into extra time.**
BELOW **Wendell Sailor, who failed to spark on the night, attempts to halt a trademark drive from England No. 8 Lawrence Dallaglio as Elton Flatley closes in as back-up.**

Johnson called his troops together. So did Gregan. The Australians had fought back tenaciously. A typical pugnacious refusal to give in. That's why they're world champions in so many sports. No need to run down the list. One person was absent from the two huddles. He took a ball and went down one end of the pitch. To practise his goal-kicking. Because practice makes a perfect 10.

When play resumed for the first of the two extra ten-minute periods, he got a chance to prove it within two minutes. 17-14. Catt was on now, bursting through the middle, making crucial tackles. This was the man whose World Cup legacy was being Jonah Lomu's doormat. Eight years on, the key figure against Wales and France was to play a vital part in securing England's historic win. Substitutes came and went. Larkham had been kicked in the mouth early on and played musical chairs with Giteau to receive constant attention. When he was on, the Wallabies looked more dangerous. Around him, legs were getting tired.

At the break, it was time to consult the rule book. If things are level, what happens? We get an extra period in which the first team to score wins. And then? Then it's a drop-kick penalty shoot-out competition. 'Imagine,' we said in the commentary box, 'if Jason Leonard has a drop kick to win the World Cup.' Oh, how we laughed.

The players were tired? What about the rest of us watching? Remembering to breathe was tricky. All about possession and no errors. Gregan a glorious grubber through. Then Tuqiri surging for the line. The crowd wrapped in hysteria. The Wallabies to win. What a tackle by Robinson. Just like that one in the match in Perth so long ago, which swung the match against the Springboks. England with a throw-in. Another mistake. Dallaglio handling on the ground. Flatley again.

The clock ticking down. The biggest audience ever for a rugby match. The biggest crowd for any game in Australia. Blah, blah. As above. Flatley's heartbeat must have been audible in Twickenham by now. What a kick! What strength of character! What a game! How could it be that with just seconds left, the scores were level again at 17-all? Jason. In all your 113 caps, you

BELOW **The world waits… Team-mates and opponents look on in anticipation as Jonny Wilkinson swings into action to make it 20-17 to England with 20 seconds left on the clock.**

ABOVE **World Champions! England's four-year odyssey ends in victory at Telstra Stadium. For Australia, the disappointment of coming within an ace of retaining their title.**
RIGHT **Elation and relief in the stands as the final whistle brings the rollercoaster to a halt at last.**

can never have had a moment like the one that could be heading your way. When did you last drop a goal, Jason?

All week the Australian papers had been talking about Jonny. The taxi drivers had been talking about him. Even the bloke in the laundrette was talking about him. The *Sydney Morning Herald* produced 'Stop Jonny' T-shirts. They posted one on the beach outside England's hotel. But how can you stop something, or someone, that has been chosen for greatness and immortality?

England win the line. Johnno drives. Jonny in the pocket. You can see him. Poised. He knows. He'd been there a few moments earlier, but the ball hadn't arrived. It did this time. Right foot. How many Premiership footballers do you know who are equally adept with both feet? A moment frozen in time. Not a roar rising to a crescendo. Silence. Broken by pandemonium.

England are the world champions. Johnno and Jonny creating the winning score, and the two of them, so often pictured either scowling or intent, are wreathed in smiles. Jonny looks like a man reborn. A defining moment in his life. He'll still keep practising. All the time. But what he wanted more than anything else has come his way. Greatness.

Meanwhile, it is still bucketing down. Johnno picks up the cup. A giant of a man and a giant of a leader. England had confounded their Aussie critics who'd called them 'Dad's Army'. Gregan gave a post-match interview and was magnificent. The Wallabies' fans responded. Beaten but proud, the green-and-gold hordes had been part of an unforgettable sporting drama. They said well done to the travelling English support. They might have said that on such a day, rugby was the winner, but they'd have hated to lapse into such cheap cliché.

Nobody does it better than Australia. Maybe they should just stage everything. The Eurovision Song Contest perhaps. And

England. They'd done it. Each and every member of the squad could say they were world champions. How many ever get the chance to say that in a lifetime? Pundits pontificated on the spin-offs for the game domestically and at large. The IRB spoke of the best World Cup of all being the catalyst for growth across the globe. Talk is cheap. Go and do something about it. You've been given the perfect springboard.

I'll mention him just once more; his surname, too, because otherwise the gag doesn't work. Wilkinson had put Australia to the sword. And at one minute to midnight on the day of the World Cup final, it was still raining. But nobody seemed to care.

FACING PAGE **Captain Fantastic. The Lions, the Six Nations Grand Slam – and now Martin Johnson lifts the Webb Ellis Cup.**
BELOW **Clive Woodward, world champion coach, contemplates rugby's holy grail.**
FOLLOWING PAGES **The Class of '03.**

Clive Woodward acknowledges the fans.

What they said...

England: Jonny Wilkinson (fly half)

"I am over the moon, you cannot describe the feeling. It is not just winning the World Cup but being part of the team and feeling that kind of togetherness and that desire and those emotions and those dreams that everyone is trying to live out. We've attacked everything full on and we've taken our fair share of hits from everyone around. But we've always believed in ourselves and we have stuck together. There has not been one argument in the whole tournament. We have pulled together and we needed that more so today than any other characteristic.

"I was always lined up to take that drop goal: but there was a bit too much pressure so Johnno took the ball up one more time which gave me a bit more space and thankfully with about ten million hours of practice under my belt, I managed just one out of four but it was the important one that went over.

"Their defence was fantastic and put a lot of pressure on me, but you can't argue with that. I had a shot at two or three earlier that I should have got, the sort of snap efforts you hope to block over, but thankfully the last one was the one that counted – but I would rather not have played that long before it went over.

"The Australians have been under as much pressure as we have, and they have survived it and they have done brilliantly. It has been an amazing campaign by them. To go through a game like the semi-final against New Zealand and come out the next week and hit us the way they did was remarkable. At times the ball went our way during the game, at times theirs, but for us to finish out on top was brilliant."

Australia: Eddie Jones (coach)

"We are shattered. The best team won on the night. We weren't quite good enough. We went very close, but just weren't good enough. I was extremely proud of the team. The guys have worked very hard, some of them for two years, some of them for twelve months. We gave ourselves the best opportunity to win the World Cup but came up short. We have worked very hard to put ourselves in the best position but were not good enough on the night. England were outstanding. They are the best team in the world. They play to their strengths. They have a very good forward pack and they have some very hard running backs. They are extremely well coached, extremely well prepared and they have a huge amount of talent in their squad. I think they have deserved what they have done in the last four years, since being knocked out in the 1999 quarter-finals. They had to play well. We certainly put them under the pump, but by the end we were not quite up to it.

"Look at our starting XV – only two of those guys, George Gregan and Steve Larkham, played in the '99 World Cup final. I'd say 80 per cent of our guys from today should be available for the next World Cup so there are some real positives for the future. This side has shown enormous resolve and it is a side the country should be proud of. The guys have lost some battles in trying to win a war and now we have lost the war as well, but I tell you what, we went down with all guns blazing."

Eddie Jones takes the strain.

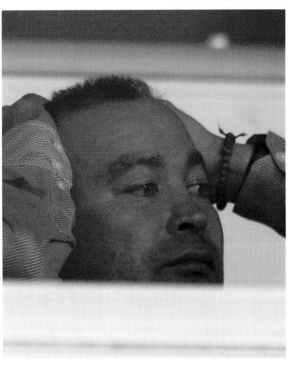

Australia: George Gregan (captain)

"Everybody is disappointed but there is a mixture of pride there. Our performance was a gutsy effort from everyone. It was a massive final that came down to the last play in extra time, so both teams did not leave anything in terms of reserve. That's all I can ask as captain of a team and I was so proud of the efforts of every one of the Wallabies.

"When Flats kicked the goal to level the score in extra time, I knew that England would drive hard at us. We needed field position but they had the ball and I could see that Jonny Wilkinson was positioning himself nicely to do what he does best. They took it forward and the rest is history. They must only be applauded for that. As for all this talk before this match of them being boring, I've always said they are very, very professional. They do what they have to do to get victories. They play to their strengths. They knew what they had to do tonight, and that is why they are world champions and they deserve to be. From an Australian's point of view you have to take your hat off to them. It has been a great experience for our young guys. They now know what it takes to win a World Cup final. Hopefully they will be on the winning side in four years' time. For me, I'm taking some annual leave now and will be making a decision on my future in the New Year."

George Gregan in reflective mood.

Clive Woodward congratulates his match winner.

England: Clive Woodward (coach)

"My first thoughts are for every single person in a white shirt in the ground. Their support has been fantastic. I just can't describe the atmosphere here. It just makes you so proud to be English. And also for the people who have been listening on the radio and watching on TV, I hope you have enjoyed it all as much as we have. I am so proud of the players and everyone involved in the team. During the match we were getting pretty cranky because we weren't playing well. We kept saying 'We're going to give this away'. We were making so many errors, but who cares! I'm not going to take any questions on how we played. We won and that's it. We have got the cup. I haven't an idea what winning the World Cup will mean in the long term. What it means now is that I have a medal round my neck and there is a big gold cup in the changing room. The story here is the fans in the stadium and the millions at home. They are just unbelievable and a big thank you from me and Martin Johnson and the boys. We couldn't have done it without that support. All I'm looking forward to at the moment is going home.

"I was very confident going into the game and I am still in shock that we had to go into injury time to win it. You just look at the win-loss record. We have lost, I think, four games in four years and I know that we have won five in a row against Australia – the last two away from home. We're on a big roll. Winning the World Cup is very important but no more than that. I like to think the current success of the national team is mirroring the success of the game at home in the Premiership. We owe a lot to all the Premiership clubs, the 12 owners and the RFU. We feel very lucky and privileged to be able to put the icing on the cake. We must keep this moment going and make sure that the current success of the team is not a blip in history."

England: Lawrence Dallaglio (No. 8)

"You have to savour the day. You have to take in the atmosphere and enjoy it with the fans. Our supporters throughout this tournament have been fantastic right from the first game against Georgia, then against South Africa and throughout the competition. They've had to listen to a lot of what has been said and written about us, but they have stuck with us and just been fantastic every time we've played. And today has been no different. They have thoroughly enjoyed themselves throughout Australia and today was a special day for them as well as for the millions of people back home."

The back row – Neil Back, Lawrence Dallaglio and Richard Hill.

England: Martin Johnson (captain)

"It has not really sunk in for me. To lose the lead the way we did in the second half was disappointing and to have to play another 20 minutes. Then to go ahead and see them get back again, that was very hard. But we knew then that we just had to get some ball. We planned the line out and what we would do from the kick-off and worked our way into a position for a drop goal – and you wouldn't want anybody else in the world to take it except Jonny. But the impact of what we've achieved has not really sunk in. It is just a fantastic achievement for all the players, for the management, for everyone involved and for all the supporters and the whole of England. Fantastic. We are just happy; we have gone the full distance and we have won it. It would have been horrible to lose, especially down here. They may call us gloaters, but they have some skill at that themselves. We have taken a lot of stick down here. It was just nice to win it and for our fans to be able to go into town, to hold their heads up high here in Sydney and say, 'Yes, we have come here and we have beaten Australia at home in a World Cup final and that takes some doing'. That achievement is pretty special."

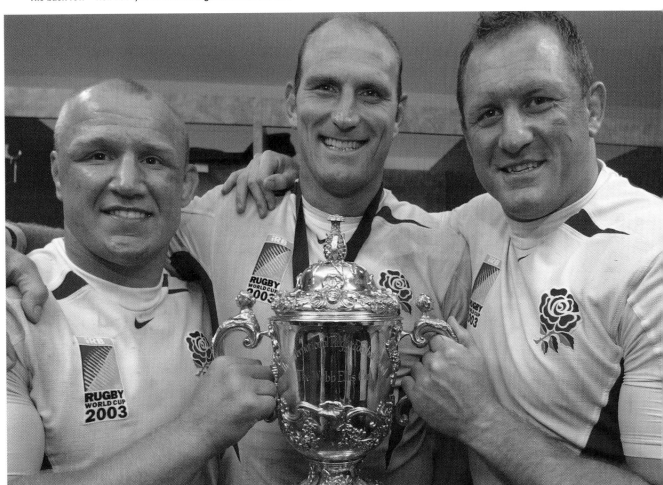

England: Ben Kay (lock)

"It is a great feeling to be a world champion. The game was not very pretty and we made a lot of mistakes, but we won it and that's what counts.

"When I dropped the ball with a try on a plate in front of me, I had visions of spending the rest of my life doing pizza adverts [like Tony Underwood after the 1995 World Cup]. So when Jonny's drop goal went over I was absolutely ecstatic."

England: Will Greenwood (centre)

"At the end I just kept shouting to Mike Catt and Jonny 'We've won the World Cup!' During the game I kept thinking of my little baby Freddie who died after living just a few minutes last year. I am not religious, but I hoped he was somewhere in the sky watching his Dad.

"I have decided it is time to stop looking after Jonny. He can manage brilliantly on his own. We have been wonderfully coached and Clive has stood by his players. They can never now take away from us the label 'World Cup Winners 2003' – just like the 1966 football boys."

England: Ben Cohen (wing)

"I can't quite find enough words to say how I feel, especially with the World Cup soccer win in 1966. It's two wins in the family. I can't believe it. It's fantastic.

"I don't think that we played particularly well in the second half. Luckily the first half held us up well. At the end of the day, it's who's in front at the end.

"I hope the fans get absolutely hammered, because we are going to!"

England: Neil Back (flanker)

"All that talk of 'Dad's Army' inspired us. We knew that in extra time they would also be very tired.

"It has been a long journey since World Cup 1999, four long years. But now we have four long years to enjoy our status as world champions. We have been rated as the world number one, but league tables mean nothing unless you prove yourself on the pitch.

"I had volunteered to be one of the drop-kickers if it came to a shoot-out. At the last knockings, I thought 'What have I let myself in for?' So, good old Jonny!"

No pizza ads for Ben Kay.

England: Matt Dawson (scrum half)

❝I don't want to try to top what we achieved here. This is a career peak. My medal will be worn for a long time and if you can find out if I'll wear it in bed, good luck. It will always be close to me. There were loads of times when I thought that we would let it slip away. We turned over ball and gave away penalties. But we knew that if we could get possession and territory we would win. I saw the eyes of all our players during the pause before extra time and knew that we were up for it.

❝I had 84 text messages on my mobile after the game, so we soon realised that passion back home had gone through the roof after the tremendous interest that we knew about earlier in the cup.

❝The atmosphere in Sydney was second to none. When it came to the vital extra time, it was not a question of whether we deserved it. We had made life difficult for ourselves and we had to earn it. We used all our experience from defeats and wins over recent seasons to scrape home. This was the culmination of at least six years' effort.❞

England: Jason Leonard (prop)

❝We could not have done it without them. There might be a trip to the palace for one or two – but let's not forget the unsung lot.

❝It was not a case of payback for losing in 1991. I am the only one still here who lost to those Wallabies in the final. They were better then. We are better now. In the scrums Trevor and Phil were doing nothing wrong, but were being penalised. When I came on we decided to give the ref nothing to penalise, with the effect that we were scrumming passively rather than aggressively. But it worked.❞

Jason, a veteran of 113 England Tests, typically paid tribute to the 'dirt-trackers'.

Jason Leonard, beaten finalist in 1991, enjoys the moment.

LOOKING BACK

Yes, the Greatest Show on Turf

ALASTAIR HIGNELL

ABOVE A tiny fraction of the 1.8 million spectators who attended RWC 2003 enjoys the Italy v Canada game at Canberra Stadium.

Australia loved the World Cup, and the World Cup loved Australia – though not quite enough to let the Wallabies keep the trophy. As long as rugby is played, Rugby World Cup 2003 will hold a special place in the memory. If the final was pure theatre, the tournament itself was pure Hollywood. Along the way to that heart-stopping climax, there were far more twists, far more sub-plots than even California's finest scriptwriters would have dared to include. In the course of several weeks, we had medical dramas, we had epic journeys, we had farce, we had David and Goliath confrontations, we had action thrillers, we had spectacular backdrops – we even had a courtroom drama. Rugby World Cup 2003 was not only sensational at the box office, it created a feel-good factor that will last for years.

The statistics are staggering. Fully 1.8 million fans poured through the turnstiles for the 48 matches, with the attendance at the final of just under 83,000 a World Cup record. A quarter of all matches played attracted crowds of more than 40,000, seven more recorded attendances of more than 30,000 and all seven at Telstra Stadium in Sydney topped the 75,000 mark. Officially, 40,000 overseas visitors arrived in 400 jumbo jets and took up a half million Australian bed nights – unofficially, with so many individuals making their own arrangements, the figures had to be much larger still.

And the spending power of World Cup fans was phenomenal. All across Australia extraordinary figures were posted. In Adelaide, for instance, it was reported that city bars reaped a bonanza of up to 30 times their regular nightly takings when the rugby circus was in town. All 12,000 hotel beds in Brisbane were taken during the weekend of the England-Wales quarter-final. The matches at Gosford resulted in a $10 million injection into the Central Coast economy. Perth welcomed more than three times the normal number of visitors, who poured more than $15 million into the Western Australia economy. New South Wales tourist minister Sandra Nori reckoned that the tournament was worth $350 million to the state, with untold future benefits as a result of New South Wales being showcased to a potential audience of 3.3 billion.

Not surprisingly, the guardians of the game, the IRB, were purring. Chief Executive Mike Miller's overriding impression was of 'a nation that decided to come out and party and did it in style,

BELOW **Spectacular backdrop. The Japanese squad train at the foot of Castle Hill, Townsville, Queensland.**

and teams that decided they wanted to go out and entertain, and did so'. With some justification, Miller could point to the fact that there were far more memorable matches in 2003 than there were in previous competitions. While the final and two semi-finals were always likely to be gripping spectacles, this time round there were so many other matches that stood out. Samoa lived up to their World Cup traditions with an extraordinary first hour against England in Melbourne. Wales stunned first New Zealand and then England with the effervescence of their attacking play. Both Scotland against Fiji and Ireland against Australia contributed mightily to nail-biting climaxes. The Japanese showed wondrous skills, and there were moments of magic from Fiji and Italy. The lesser lights enjoyed their day in the sun. The Georgia-Uruguay match and Namibia's contest with Romania in Launceston were mini-finals. According to Miller there were just two genuine mismatches – Australia's 142-0 thrashing of Namibia and England's 111-13 victory over Uruguay.

That said, there were no real surprises in Rugby World Cup 2003. The eight seeded teams reached the quarter-finals, and the team ranked number one in the world lifted the Webb Ellis trophy. The only real shock to the established order of things was Australia's semi-final win over New Zealand. Miller is not too concerned about predictability. 'This is a hard, unforgiving game and it is very difficult for lesser teams to compete with the more professionally prepared outfits for the full 80 minutes, but let's not forget that in soccer it tends to be the same teams that always win the big trophies. We've only been professional for eight years. We've come a long way in the time and this World Cup reflects that success. Looking forward, I'm sure we will invest wisely the money that we have earned from this tournament to continue the global growth of the game.'

And that theme was echoed by Wallaby coach Eddie Jones in his post-final press conference: 'The World Cup has been an outstanding success but I think that if you look at teams ranked 10 to 16, they were all in a position when they could have won games against teams ranked in the top eight, so that's pretty healthy. I think the IRB needs to put some effort into developing those teams because they are the countries that can make a legitimate and significant improvement over the next four years and be the sort of sides that can actually challenge for quarter-final places. If you look ahead to the 2007 World Cup, you would want all of the top 16 sides to be genuine quarter-final candidates. The target for the teams ranked 17 to 20, who struggled a bit in this World Cup, would be for them to get into the position that at some point in a match against teams above them, they would have a genuine chance of victory.'

The IRB has acknowledged that the problem of the developing nations needs to be addressed. Sides like Samoa, Fiji, Tonga and Canada were not at full strength for the tournament because several of their leading players chose to stick with more lucrative club contracts. Samoa coach John Boe made a heartfelt plea to the governing body to do something quickly because he felt that otherwise the drain on his country's playing resources would become irreversible and this would be Samoa's last World Cup. As a result, the newly elected chairman of the IRB, Syd Miller, is heading up a think tank to discuss the best way of helping out the second-tier nations.

Otherwise, as the game gets more complex, as training and preparation become more refined, the rich become richer and the gap to the poor becomes unbridgeable. England, like Australia, New Zealand and South Africa, throw millions of pounds at their World Cup efforts. England are now accompanied by a team of 18 specialists, including a lawyer – who earned his corn during the 'Luger-gate' affair – and a cook. They use anti-surveillance equipment as a matter of course and are prepared to do whatever it takes to protect their assets and to keep their edge. No other side, you suspect, would be prepared to fly two players, Martyn Wood and Austin Healey, around the world as cover for a temporary injury crisis, before sending them straight home again.

As far as Woodward, and every England fan, is concerned, the end has justified the means. While the true value of England's capture of rugby's greatest prize has still to be assessed, its influence on the game of rugby is already being felt. The success of England's rolling-maul tactics, dubbed the 'truck and trailer' by Australian commentators, will interest the lawmakers when they meet in early 2004 just as much as the decoy runners employed by the Wallabies. The influence of dropped goals on the course of rugby matches will also be examined, with real consideration being given to the idea of reducing the points awarded.

And England's achievement in breaking the southern hemisphere stranglehold on the game is bound to have far-reaching consequences for rugby. As Eddie Jones put it, 'What has happened over the last four years since Australia won the World Cup is that northern hemisphere sides, and in particular France and England, have really honed their technical and tactical skills in the set piece. They have certainly gone ahead of the southern hemisphere countries in that way. I think you saw that with England's outstanding competence in that area. They've taken the game forward in a different way. We took the game forward through continuity. They've taken it forward through contest. Now the challenge is which country rather than which hemisphere is to accomplish the next cycle of development.'

And so to France for 2007. The French Federation had a strong presence in Sydney for the final two weeks of this World Cup and know they will have to pull some marketing rabbits out of the hat to match the Australian effort. England will have to find a new team if they are to emulate the achievements of Martin Johnson and his men. After 'choking' yet again, New Zealand will be even more determined to gain some tangible reward. South Africa will be stronger too, while France at home will take some stopping. That is the way of sport. Sights are so swiftly set on the future that present achievements can be quickly overlooked. Take time, therefore, to reflect on a great World Cup, a great World Cup final and worthy world champions. This year belongs to England.

BELOW **Bath's Martyn Wood arrives at Perth as possible scrum half cover for England. In the event, his services were not required and he returned home without joining the squad.**

TIME FLIES

HIGHLIGHTS

Player of the Tournament – **Jonny Wilkinson**

EDDIE BUTLER

There wasn't really any chance that Jonny Wilkinson would go completely bonkers in Australia. It was just that for a time it seemed that he couldn't help but climb on board the couch and tell us all about his anxiety and his goals and the pressure he put on himself, and how he fast-forwarded through the positive and homed in on the negative.

England at that time were not playing particularly well. They had seen off South Africa but were severely rattled by Samoa. Wilkinson had not missed a shot at goal in the first two games but was suddenly a bit off-target. He was not dropping the ball on to his foot for his punts at the right angle. He was hesitant on the end of his half-back partners' service. Most obvious was a new nervous habit. His left foot had developed almost a spasm, a tic as he prepared himself for his place-kicks.

In his column for *The Times* he explained this very rationally. This was a routine to make his foot what he called 'hard'. A soft foot does not make a good contact with the ball. It has to be hard. Fine, but the swirling and tapping of the foot were growing more and more exaggerated, and at the top end of his body he was looking quite dreadful. His face was drawn, pinched, baggy-eyed. Hell, he was looking old. Five years after his international career began, in England's 0-76 thrashing in Brisbane by the Wallabies, was he heading for the scrap heap, at the tender age of 24? As he presented himself, solo, on his couch at the press conferences the questions would not go away. Was he turning dippy?

Against Wales in the quarter-final he scored 23 points. Hardly the work of a madman. But England had again been below par in the first half. A penalty had been missed; a dropped goal had been missed. And now he was burying himself in rucks. He described his contribution thus: 'Working your guts out, running till it hurts and then clearing out rucks, challenging for the ball and getting off the ball.' His coach came to his defence, calling him a wonderful rucker. But did Clive Woodward really want his playmaker up to his shoulders in bodies when there was a game to run? Should his general not be out of harm's way?

They sent for help. His dad arrived in Australia. Rob Andrew, his coach and mentor at Newcastle, arrived to work for BBC Radio Five Live. And Mike Catt arrived at inside centre for the

RIGHT **Nothing more to prove. A smiling, relaxed-looking Jonny Wilkinson – World Cup winner and player of the tournament.**

second half of that quarter-final against Wales. Suddenly there was a sounding board alongside him, a talker, a communicator. England powered their way back into the game. Over went a stream of penalties. Wilkinson stopped going solo at press conferences. Oh, people still asked him about his flakiness, but he was now flanked by the likes of Martin Johnson and Lawrence Dallaglio. These bodyguards offered silent support, deflected the heat and sniggered whenever the boy threatened to go wonky.

In the next game he was sublime. In a virtuoso semi-final performance against France he kicked three dropped goals and five penalties. And England were through to the final. He won his personal duel with Frederic Michalak, the outside half who had been making all the running in the World Cup up to that point with the daring and the perfection of his play. The French back row, who were primed to seize on the slightest weakness, laid barely a finger on Wilkinson, despite the rain and the filth of the night. This was not meant to be a night for twitchy outside halves. But the bags under the eyes had gone. Calm authority was restored.

After the pool game against South Africa, way back in time and way across the country in Perth, *The Australian* newspaper had taunted England with a full-page picture of Wilkinson and the question: 'Is that all you've got?' The reply was still the same: It may be more than enough.

It remains to be seen whether Wilkinson's public outpouring of his inner workings was a genuine attempt to offer something more than the usual nonsense trotted out at press conferences. Or whether he got caught in a thread which became a bit of a tangle. You start talking about the simple things of the game, how you prepare and how you concentrate and analyse your performance. And you just reveal a little bit too much of the obsessive in you. Of the teenager who disappeared for hours – days – at a time, practising his kicking, his kicking, his kicking.

Or was he just knackered, like any other player at the World Cup? He had every right to look exhausted at that time, for this was the stage of the competition when training was at maximum intensity. Every player, even one who strives to be the best that has ever existed, is entitled to miss the odd pop at goal, or slice the occasional clearance to touch. Or make the odd mistake when it comes to those split-second decisions about whether to stay out of contact or go in and heave some bodies about.

But the strange period of the confessional and the loss of form and the stressed eyes may not have been mere coincidence. It may have been a genuine career crisis. He came through it. He pulled himself out of the mini-slump, and his team adjusted to help him through. He made one tackle on Imanol Harinordoquy that had cold-hearted sanity stamped all over it. He dropped goals with his right foot and his left. It makes the Wilkinson legend only grow, knowing that he can suffer. That he came through. The master was restored at his workbench. Boy Bonkers had given way to Boy Wonder. It was good to see him back.

Rugby World Cup 2003 – **World XV**

ROB ANDREW AND GARETH CHILCOTT

It's difficult to pick a definitive World XV with 20 countries playing a total of 48 matches, especially when 12 of those teams exit stage left at the quarter-final stage. Several players caught the eye in the pool games, but they had to be really outstanding to be considered for the final XV if they played in teams that failed to reach the quarter-finals. Many of the pool matches were one-sided affairs, and it would be unfair to select someone who performed well in one tough pool game but who was in a side that failed to reach the much more demanding knockout stages.

Hence it was felt that well though many of the Samoans played – especially Brian Lima in the centre and Semo Setiti at No. 8 – they could only merit honourable mentions in despatches and an acknowledgement that if a World XV had been selected before the quarter-finals both these two would have been included. Much the same applies to some of the Argentinian forwards, principally the front row, and to the Puma scrum half, Agustin Pichot. So from the 12 teams who were eliminated after the pool stage, only one player has made the World XV – Caucau, and that is because he was sensational on the wing for Fiji.

Having established these criteria, we asked former England and Lions fly half Rob Andrew to select the backs, and former England and Lions prop Gareth Chilcott to pick the forwards.

The Backs – Rob Andrew

Three full backs all played well, but my vote goes to Mils Muliaina of New Zealand. He was the best attacking full back in the tournament, and he was also rock-solid in defence. Next best came Mat Rogers of Australia and Josh Lewsey of England.

Several wings captured the headlines, but one certainly had to be the flying Fijian – Caucau. He can play on the right or the left, so that meant we could then pick the next-best player no matter which side he played. Wendell Sailor of Australia had his moments but was not the finished article. The same can be said of Joe Rokocoko of New Zealand and Lote Tuqiri of Australia. The French wings Aurelien Rougerie and Christophe Dominici were very good until they disintegrated in the semi-final against England. Shane Williams had a couple of brilliant matches, but over the whole six weeks of the World Cup my vote goes to Doug Howlett of New Zealand.

In the centre I had no problem putting down the name of Brian O'Driscoll right away. He had a tremendous tournament and earned the No. 13 jersey ahead of a group of good players, including England's Will Greenwood and Tony Marsh of France.

It was hard to pick the other centre, and my shortlist included Aaron Mauger of New Zealand, Mike Catt of England, who sadly played only a limited role in the knockout stages but looked terrific, Iestyn Harris of Wales, and Elton Flatley of Australia. In the end, though, I have gone for Stirling Mortlock of Australia to partner O'Driscoll.

Fly half is very easy – Jonny Wilkinson. Not always at his very best, he still remains far and away the best fly half in the world. Carlos Spencer and Stephen Larkham had their moments. Similarly at scrum half, I have no hesitation in choosing Justin Marshall of New Zealand. Several others deserve a mention, notably Matt Dawson of England, Fabien Galthie of France and George Gregan of Australia.

I am very happy that if Gareth Chilcott can pick a pack to win a decent share of possession this back division will shine.

BELOW Honourable mention. Argentina's scrum half Agustin Pichot in action in the Pool A match against Ireland at the Adelaide Oval.

ABOVE **Malcolm O'Kelly rises to gather for Ireland at a line out during the quarter-final against France at Telstra Dome. The Irish lock gets the nod to partner Martin Johnson in the second row.**

The Pack – Gareth Chilcott

The front row has probably been the most difficult because I have found it hard to find two props who stood out head and shoulders above the rest. At loose-head prop I narrowed it down to three – Tom Smith of Scotland, Jean Jacques Crenca of France and Kees Meeuws of New Zealand. It was hard to go for Meeuws because he was used more as an impact player and so he didn't start most games. If he wasn't good enough for the All Blacks, he couldn't be good enough for our World XV.

Crenca was in the lead going into the semi-finals, but he disappointed against England, and so I have chosen Smith. He scrummaged well right through the tournament and was always outstanding in open play. At tight-head I have gone for Phil Vickery ahead of Sylvain Marconnet of France. Vickery, like Tom Smith, is very mobile in the open as well as being a good scrummager.

At hooker I have no hesitation in choosing Ireland's Keith Wood. He has been in great form since recovering from a long-term injury and he had a wonderful run in the World Cup before Ireland lost to France and Wood announced his retirement. His nearest challenger was Keven Mealamu of New Zealand.

At lock Martin Johnson of England was in a class of his own, and it would be impossible to choose anyone else to captain the World XV. Chris Jack of New Zealand and Justin Harrison of Australia played well, but they were a long way short of the standard set by Martin Johnson. To partner Johnson I have given preference by the narrowest of margins to Malcolm O'Kelly of Ireland, just ahead of Ben Kay of England, Victor Matfield of South Africa and Nathan Sharpe of Australia.

There were several good No. 8s who had to be considered, notably Jerry Collins of New Zealand, Imanol Harinordoquy of France, Lawrence Dallaglio of England and David Lyons of Australia. However, the vote goes to Simon Taylor of Scotland, who was absolutely tremendous in every match he played, especially as he was fighting a tough cause in a losing pack.

There were a lot of very good flankers. It was hard to leave out multi-talented players like Joe Van Niekerk of South Africa, Richie McCaw of New Zealand, Serge Betsen of France and George Smith of Australia. Even though England's Richard Hill only played in three matches, he proved what a great forward he is and he wins the No. 6 jersey. For consistently good performances of the very highest standard, Wallaby Phil Waugh completes the back row.

In a tournament which was more notable for team performances than brilliant individuals, this is a balanced side which should be able to execute any game plan and operate effectively in all conditions.

The Highs and the Lows

CHRIS JONES

As Australian prop Ben Darwin lay on the pitch after a scrum in the titanic semi-final against New Zealand he had no feeling below his neck. It is impossible for anyone who has never faced the threat of paralysis to truly understand the panic that engulfed him at that moment. It should have been one of the most memorable days of his young life. A semi-final victory over New Zealand in front of an adoring Sydney rugby public with his family and friends there to witness his part in the triumph. Instead, they had to watch as a golf cart carried his immobile body to the dressing rooms.

The only boost Darwin got at this point was the jolting sensations of feelings starting to return to his hands and legs. It was a blessed relief, but he was still in real trouble. Less than a week later, though, Darwin returned to the same Telstra Stadium, kitted out in his team blazer and wearing a neck support. He had a prolapsed disc that required surgery and careful rehabilitation to allow him to keep playing rugby, but he was upright and wanted to show his team-mates he was fit to back them to the hilt against England in the final. His team-mates wanted him there, too, and for the Wallaby players, the news that Darwin would be present for the final was a massive boost.

Darwin's injury was a major low at RWC 2003. Yet while the damage to the Wallaby's neck dominated the story, there was another side to the incident. Kees Meeuws, the burly All Black prop, had been pushing with all his might into Darwin when he heard him shout 'neck, neck, neck'; he stopped shoving. Just imagine that for a moment. You are fired up for a World Cup semi, adrenalin pumping and then you just stop. Something inside Meeuws clicked in. It was the realisation that a fellow front-row forward had used the word that they all fear – 'neck'. Rugby is brutal enough without the risk of serious injury when it can be avoided, and avoid it is exactly what Meeuws did. He took away the pressure that was hurting his opposite number and saved him from further damage. It was one of the great highs of the World Cup; maybe one of the great sporting moments of all time.

It came at a World Cup that restored your faith in the game and that proved, once and for all, that the tournament must be staged in just one country to generate real interest. As with so many things at this World Cup, you couldn't fault the organisers for orginality. Take the use of music to greet tries. Greg Bowman, Managing and Creative Director, said, 'After listening to literally thousands and thousands of tracks we created musical packages that will ignite spectators and lift the performance of the players at every match.' As a result the events people came up with this list for the home nations – England: 'Let Me Entertain You', 'Swing Low'; Ireland: 'Jackie Wilson', 'Elevation', 'Beautiful Day'; Scotland: '500 Miles', 'I'm On My Way; Wales: 'If I Only Knew', 'Burning Down the House', 'Delilah'. For Welsh fans it was wholly appropriate that 'Delilah' should be top of the pops, and thanks to the resurgence that saw pride restored in defeat by New Zealand and England, the Tom Jones standard was belted out with added vigour.

While Sydney became the heart of the tournament for the final two weeks, the real pulse was to be found in Tasmania. Highs don't come any better than the one neutral rugby fans enjoyed when Launceston staged the Namibia v Romania match. It appeared to be a ludicrous idea – take 30 players none of the

BELOW **Upright and mobile after his brush with tragedy, Australia prop Ben Darwin (centre) was at the World Cup final to throw his support behind his team-mates.**

locals had ever heard of, from countries they probably couldn't find on the map, and ask them to turn out in their thousands on a cold and wet evening. Yet it was at places like Launceston that Rugby World Cup 2003 crossed the barriers many expected to turn the tournament into a minority event. There were 15,000 in the crowd with faces painted in the national colours of the two teams, and both sides did a lap of honour at the end.

High up on the Queensland coast, the people of Townsville found their town the focal point for hordes of Scottish supporters and responded by adopting Japan. A local chef fed the Japanese with rice flown in from their homeland, while the fans turned up in sumo wrestling garb. We were also treated to the sight of a Japanese supporter in full samurai kit playing 'Waltzing Matilda' on the bagpipes. How do you top that? On the pitch Japan showed they could now compete at the very highest level, but you got the impression – as so often in the pool stages – that the locals were just happy both teams turned up to help make the party go with a bang.

The real battle of the minnows happened in Sydney, where 30,000 watched Uruguay defeat Georgia. It was an amazing crowd for a 'dead' game in terms of who won the pool, but that wasn't the point. Uruguay captain Diego Aguirre had his moment of World Cup glory and it will live with him and his amateur players for the rest of their lives. Until that point, Uruguayan rugby was best known for the 1970s air crash that became the film *Alive!*, chronicling the ordeal of the passengers, who were forced to eat their dead rugby club team-mates to survive. The tournament has given Uruguayan rugby a new positive reference point.

While the fans and the players gained the most credit, there was also applause for Brisbane's Suncorp Stadium. The local government spent more than £120 million turning this rugby league centre of excellence into a stadium fit to stage huge World Cup matches, and they even paid out another £700,000 to make sure the pitch was perfect. It was, and the Suncorp was by some way the best rugby venue in the tournament.

Of course with all these highs there had to be lows. Many revolved around indiscipline and injuries, with Martin Leslie of Scotland ending up with an eight-week ban for use of the knee against the USA and Rupeni Caucaunibuca also collecting a ban for throwing a punch against France – after scoring one of the tries of the tournament. Al Charron, the veteran Canadian captain, left his final match for his country on a stretcher thanks to a tackle by Tonga's Pierre Hola, who didn't use his arms. Charron needed surgery to repair a cut in his mouth and was denied the kind of farewell his team-mates and the people of Wollongong wanted to give this great servant of Canadian rugby.

Scotland had some very public lows off the field, with reports of drinking binges and verbal fights between their players; and then there were the hotel changes. The first move was due to the arrival of Hell's Angels in the same town, and then they were unhappy that a wedding reception was taking place in their next hotel. At least they redeemed themselves with a performance of true grit against Australia in the quarter-finals to help the retiring pair of captain Bryan Redpath and wing Kenny Logan head into the sunset with some pride restored.

Georgia wanted to prove that a new 'baby' had been born to the international rugby family and took the unusual step of wetting the infant's head before we had actually seen it. Based in Perth, the Georgians gained a 500-strong paid-up supporters group who used their subscriptions to help a local hospital for children and one in Tbilisi. The Georgians, most of whom play in France, supped ale with the locals on arrival and continued to have a good time throughout. Their only regret was losing that final pool game to a Uruguay side lower in the world rankings.

With Samoa you just get highs. They have the best team spirit of any nation despite being robbed of countless first-choice players who weren't released from club and provincial contracts in New Zealand and Europe. Yet they still managed to give England an almighty fright. Coach John Boe and assistant Michael Jones were exemplary ambassadors for the sport, and captain Semo Sititi, who plies his trade in Edinburgh, took time off work, lost money and led his country with humility and outstanding play. Meanwhile, Brian 'The Chiropractor' Lima put in the best hit of the tournament, knocking South Africa's Derick Hougaard senseless. It was Lima's fourth World Cup. Hougaard was eight years old when the Samoan played in his first.

If you wanted to learn about playing against the odds, then all you had to do was sit down with Namibia's Rudi van Vuuren. He became the first player to turn out in World Cup rugby and cricket tournaments in the same year by making his appearance in the last ten minutes at Launceston. In cricket he is a medium-pace bowler and lower-order batsman; in rugby, a utility back. He then returned home to pick up the work that had been put on hold for both sporting dreams to be realised.

The World Cup could have been a nightmare for Italy coach John Kirwan, who was told two pool wins would keep him in a job and anything less would result in the sack. His good humour and language skills belied the pressure he was under, and Kirwan and Italy emerged stronger for the experience.

At Rugby World Cup 2003 there were so many happy dreams that the nightmares were easily forgotten. Now, bring on RWC 2007 in France!

The things we do for love ... and rugby

JILL DOUGLAS

England's win over South Africa in Perth was the perfect wedding gift for Janice and Chris Brignull. The two rugby fans were married in the city's Kings Park just a few hours before kick-off. It was a memorable day for the happy couple and the dozens of England fans who joined in the fun before heading off to the Subiaco Oval for the match. And it was made all the more special because the ceremony was only finalised a couple of days earlier, when Chris, 22, was finally released to fly down from Iraq, where he was serving with the British Army in Basra.

'It has been the trip of a lifetime,' said Chris, a Sapper with the 38th Engineers. His fiancée, 26-year-old Janice Jones, won a trip to see the match with England team sponsor O_2. The couple hoped to combine the Australian holiday with their wedding, but Chris had his request for leave denied.

'I was gutted. I just moped around in Basra. I couldn't eat or anything,' said the young soldier. His fiancée was equally disappointed. 'It was a fantastic opportunity and I just wanted to share it with Chris,' said Janice, who works at the Bethlem Royal Hospital in Plumstead. 'When I mentioned it down here, O_2 said they'd try to help, but I still didn't know if it would be possible. There were so many obstacles. It's obviously fate that we were supposed to get married here on Saturday. And as it turns out, it's been a good omen for the England team.'

Paul Samuels, head of sponsorship at O_2, contacted Chris's captain in Iraq and managed to secure him just a week's leave to allow him to fly down to Perth. But Chris had a few days of anxious waiting to hear if he could go. 'I didn't dare believe it. I was trying hard not to get my hopes up. The lads in the squadron said I could only go if I could arrange flights for them too, so they could come to my stag night.'

The couple's next hurdle was obtaining the necessary permission to go through with the wedding. Normally you must be resident in the country for 30 days to marry in Australia, but the authorities entered into the spirit of the occasion and waived the rule, which they are able to do in special circumstances.

Then a venue had to be found. 'I became a wedding organiser,' said O_2's Paul Samuels. 'But we managed to book Kings Park, a beautiful outdoor venue looking out over the Swan River and the city. All our other competition winners joined in and wore their England shirts to the wedding. It really was a fantastic day and a very special one for Chris and Janice.'

The RFU also helped out, providing a couple of tickets for the big match. And of course the team joined in by providing the victory over South Africa to round off a perfect day.

ABOVE LEFT **Chris and Janice, and the Perth skyline.**
BELOW **Two others who enjoyed the trip of a lifetime were Belinda Evans and James Laing. They were chosen to represent England in the world choir at the opening ceremony and led the singing of the National Anthem before every England game.**

Statistics

Rugby World Cup 1987-2003

Highest scores:
145	New Zealand v Japan (Bloemfontein, 1995)
142	Australia v Namibia (Adelaide, 2003)
111	England v Uruguay (Brisbane, 2003)

Biggest winning margin:
142	Australia v Namibia (Adelaide, 2003)
128	New Zealand v Japan (Bloemfontein, 1995)
98	England v Uruguay (Brisbane, 2003)
98	New Zealand v Italy (Huddersfield, 1999)

Most points by a player in a match:
45	Simon Culhane (New Zealand v Japan, 1995)
44	Gavin Hastings (Scotland v Ivory Coast, 1995)
42	Mat Rogers (Australia v Namibia, 2003)

Most tries by a player in a match:
6	Marc Ellis (New Zealand v Japan, 1995)
5	Chris Latham (Australia v Namibia, 2003)
5	Josh Lewsey (England v Uruguay, 2003)
4	Ieuan Evans (Wales v Canada, 1987)
	John Gallagher (New Zealand v Fiji, 1987)
	Craig Green (New Zealand v Fiji, 1987)
	Gavin Hastings (Scotland v Ivory Coast, 1995)
	Jonah Lomu (New Zealand v England, 1995)
	Brian Robinson (Ireland v Zimbabwe, 1991)
	Chester Williams (South Africa v W. Samoa, 1995)
	Keith Wood (Ireland v USA, 1999)
	Mils Muliaina (New Zealand v Canada, 2003)

Most points in one tournament:
126	Grant Fox (New Zealand, 1987)
113	Jonny Wilkinson (England, 2003)
112	Thierry Lacroix (France, 1995)

Leading aggregate World Cup scorers:
227	Gavin Hastings (Scotland, 1987, 1991, 1995)
195	Michael Lynagh (Australia, 1987, 1991, 1995)
182	Jonny Wilkinson (England, 1999, 2003)

Most tries in World Cups:
15	Jonah Lomu (New Zealand, 1995, 1999)
11	Rory Underwood (England, 1987, 1991, 1995)
10	David Campese (Australia, 1987, 1991, 1995)

Most tries in one tournament:
8	Jonah Lomu (New Zealand, 1999)
7	Marc Ellis (New Zealand, 1995)
	Jonah Lomu (New Zealand, 1995)
	Doug Howlett (New Zealand, 2003)
	Mils Muliaina (New Zealand, 2003)

Most tries in a match by a team:
22	Australia v Namibia (Adelaide, 2003)
21	New Zealand v Japan (Bloemfontein, 1995)

Most penalty goals in World Cups:
39	Jonny Wilkinson (England, 1999, 2003)
35	Gonzalo Quesada (Argentina, 1999, 2003)
33	Andrew Mehrtens (New Zealand, 1995, 1999)

Most penalty goals in one tournament:
31	Gonzalo Quesada (Argentina, 1999)
26	Thierry Lacroix (France, 1995)
23	Jonny Wilkinson (England, 2003)

Most conversions in World Cups:
39	Gavin Hastings (Scotland, 1987, 1991, 1995)
37	Grant Fox (New Zealand, 1987, 1991)
36	Michael Lynagh (Australia, 1987, 1991, 1995)

Most conversions in one tournament:
30	Grant Fox (New Zealand, 1987)
20	Michael Lynagh (Australia, 1987)
	Simon Culhane (New Zealand, 1995)
	Leon MacDonald (New Zealand, 2003)

Most dropped goals in World Cups:
8	Jonny Wilkinson (England, 1999, 2003)
6	Jannie de Beer (South Africa, 1999)
5	Rob Andrew (England, 1987, 1991, 1995)

Most dropped goals in one tournament:
8	Jonny Wilkinson (England, 2003)
6	Jannie de Beer (South Africa, 1999)

Rugby World Cup 2003

Leading points scorers

Player	Team	Points	Tries	Cons	Pens	DG
Jonny Wilkinson	England	113	0	10	23	8
Frederic Michalak	France	103	2	18	18	1
Elton Flatley	Australia	100	1	16	21	0
Leon MacDonald	New Zealand	75	4	20	5	0
Chris Paterson	Scotland	71	3	7	13	1
Mat Rogers	Australia	57	5	16	0	0
Mike Hercus	United States	51	2	7	9	0
Rima Wakarua	Italy	50	0	4	14	0
Earl Va'a	Samoa	49	1	10	8	0
Daniel Carter	New Zealand	48	2	19	0	0
Derick Hougaard	South Africa	48	2	10	5	1
Nicky Little	Fiji	45	0	6	11	0
Toru Kurihara	Japan	40	1	4	9	0
Stephen Jones	Wales	36	1	5	7	0
Doug Howlett	New Zealand	35	7	0	0	0
Mils Muliaina	New Zealand	35	7	0	0	0
Gonzalo Quesada	Argentina	33	0	9	4	1
Paul Grayson	England	30	0	15	0	0
Iestyn Harris	Wales	30	0	9	4	0
Ronan O'Gara	Ireland	30	0	9	4	0
Joe Rokocoko	New Zealand	30	6	0	0	0
David Humphreys	Ireland	29	0	7	5	0
Will Greenwood	England	25	5	0	0	0
Chris Latham	Australia	25	5	0	0	0
Josh Lewsey	England	25	5	0	0	0
Carlos Spencer	New Zealand	25	4	1	1	0
Lote Tuqiri	Australia	25	5	0	0	0
Paliko Jimsheladze	Georgia	23	0	1	6	1
Ionut Tofan	Romania	23	0	4	5	0
Pablo Bouza	Argentina	20	4	0	0	0
Christophe Dominici	France	20	4	0	0	0
Martin Gaitan	Argentina	20	4	0	0	0
Matt Giteau	Australia	20	4	0	0	0
Louis Koen	South Africa	20	0	7	2	0
Stirling Mortlock	Australia	20	4	0	0	0
Caleb Ralph	New Zealand	20	4	0	0	0
Jason Robinson	England	20	4	0	0	0

Most tries

Player	Team	Tries
Doug Howlett	New Zealand	7
Mils Muliaina	New Zealand	7
Joe Rokocoko	New Zealand	6
Will Greenwood	England	5
Chris Latham	Australia	5
Josh Lewsey	England	5
Mat Rogers	Australia	5
Lote Tuqiri	Australia	5
Christophe Dominici	France	4
Martin Gaitan	Argentina	4
Matt Giteau	Australia	4
Stirling Mortlock	Australia	4
Leon MacDonald	New Zealand	4
Caleb Ralph	New Zealand	4
Jason Robinson	England	4
Carlos Spencer	New Zealand	4

Most penalty goals

Player	Team	Penalties
Jonny Wilkinson	England	23
Elton Flatley	Australia	21
Frederic Michalak	France	18
Rima Wakarua	Italy	14
Chris Paterson	Scotland	13
Nicky Little	Fiji	11
Mike Hercus	USA	9
Toru Kurihara	Japan	9
Earl Va'a	Samoa	8
Stephen Jones	Wales	7
Paliko Jimsheladze	Georgia	6
Leon MacDonald	New Zealand	5
Derick Hougaard	South Africa	5
David Humphreys	Ireland	5
Ionut Tofan	Romania	5
Jared Barker	Canada	5

Most conversions

Player	Team	Conversions
Leon MacDonald	New Zealand	20
Daniel Carter	New Zealand	19
Frederic Michalak	France	18
Elton Flatley	Australia	16
Mat Rogers	Australia	16

Dropped goals

Player	Team	Dropped Goals
Jonny Wilkinson	England	8
Dmitri Yachvili	France	2
Nicolas Brusque	France	1
Ignacio Corleto	Argentina	1
George Gregan	Australia	1
Derick Hougaard	South Africa	1
Paliko Jimsheladze	Georgia	1
Aaron Mauger	New Zealand	1
Frederic Michalak	France	1
Andrew Miller	Japan	1
Brian O'Driscoll	Ireland	1
Chris Paterson	Scotland	1
Gonzalo Quesada	Argentina	1
Bob Ross	Canada	1
Martyn Williams	Wales	1

Tries by country

New Zealand	52	Fiji	10
Australia	43	USA	9
England	36	Romania	8
France	29	Tonga	7
South Africa	27	Japan	6
Ireland	20	Uruguay	6
Argentina	18	Italy	5
Samoa	18	Canada	4
Wales	17	Namibia	4
Scotland	12	Georgia	1

Pool A

1 10/10/2003 — Telstra Stadium

Australia: 24	Argentina: 8
Tries: Sailor, Roff	Tries: Corleto
Cons: Flatley	Pens: F. Contepomi
Pens: Flatley (4)	
15 Mat Rogers	15 Ignacio Corleto
14 Wendell Sailor	14 J. M. Nunez Piossek
13 Matt Burke	13 Manuel Contepomi
12 Elton Flatley	12 Jose Orengo
11 Joe Roff	11 Diego Albanese
10 Stephen Larkham	10 Felipe Contepomi
9 George Gregan	9 Agustin Pichot
1 Bill Young	1 Roberto Grau
2 Brendan Cannon	2 Mario Ledesma
3 Al Baxter	3 Omar Hasan
4 David Giffin	4 I. Fernandez Lobbe
5 Nathan Sharpe	5 Patricio Albacete
6 George Smith	6 Santiago Phelan
7 Phil Waugh	7 Rolando Martin
8 David Lyons	8 Gonzalo Longo
16 Jeremy Paul*	16 Federico Mendez
17 Ben Darwin*	17 Mauricio Reggiardo*
18 Daniel Vickerman*	18 Rimas Alvarez
19 Matt Cockbain*	19 Martin Durand*
20 Chris Whitaker*	20 N. Fernandez Miranda
21 Matt Giteau*	21 Gonzalo Quesada
22 Lote Tuqiri*	22 Juan Hernandez*
Referee Paul Honiss	* = replacement used

3 11/10/2003 — Central Coast Sdm

Ireland 45	Romania 17
Tries: Hickie (2), Horgan, Wood, Costello	Tries: Maftei, pen try
Cons: Humphreys (3), O'Gara	Cons: Tofan, Andrei
Pens: Humphreys (4)	Pens: Tofan
15 Girvan Dempsey	15 Danut Dumbrava
14 Shane Horgan	14 Cristian Sauan
13 Brian O'Driscoll	13 Valentin Maftei
12 Kevin Maggs	12 Romeo Gontineac
11 Denis Hickie	11 Gabriel Brezoianu
10 David Humphreys	10 Ionut Tofan
9 Peter Stringer	9 Lucian Sirbu
1 Marcus Horan	1 Petru Balan
2 Keith Wood	2 Razvan Mavrodin
3 Reggie Corrigan	3 Marcel Socaciu
4 Malcolm O'Kelly	4 Sorin Socol
5 Paul O'Connell	5 Augustin Petrichei
6 Victor Costello	6 George Chiriac
7 Keith Gleeson	7 Ovidiu Tonita
8 Anthony Foley	8 Cristian Petre
16 Shane Byrne*	16 Petrisor Toderasc*
17 John Hayes*	17 Cezar Popescu*
18 D. O'Callaghan*	18 Marian Tudori*
19 Alan Quinlan*	19 Marius Niculai*
20 Guy Easterby*	20 Iulian Andrei*
21 Ronan O'Gara*	21 Mihai Vioreanu*
22 John Kelly*	22 Ioan Teodorescu*
Referee Jonathan Kaplan	

9 14/10/2003 — Central Coast Sdm

Argentina 67	Namibia 14
Tries: Gaitan (3), Bouza (2), Mendez, N. Fernandez Miranda, J. Fernandez Miranda, pen tries (2)	Tries: Grobler, Husselman
Cons: Quesada (7)	Cons: Wessels (2)
Pens: Quesada	
15 Juan Hernandez	15 Jurie Booysen
14 Hernan Senillosa	14 Deon Mouton
13 Martin Gaitan	13 Du Preez Grobler
12 J. Fernandez Miranda	12 Corne Powell
11 Diego Albanese	11 Melrick Africa
10 Gonzalo Quesada	10 Emile Wessels
9 N. Fernandez Miranda	9 Hakkies Husselman
1 Mauricio Reggiardo	1 Kees Lensing
2 Federico Mendez	2 Johannes Meyer
3 Martin Scelzo	3 Neil du Toit
4 Pedro Sporleder	4 Heino Senekal
5 Rimas Alvarez	5 Eben Isaacs
6 Martin Durand	6 Schalk van der Merwe
7 Lucas Ostiglia	7 Herman Lintvelt
8 Pablo Bouza	8 Sean Furter
16 Mario Ledesma*	16 Cor Van Tonder
17 Rodrigo Roncero*	17 Andries Blaauw*
18 Patricio Albacete	18 Wolfie Duvenhage*
19 I. Fernandez Lobbe*	19 Jurgens van Lill*
20 Agustin Pichot	20 Ronaldo Pedro*
21 Felipe Contepomi*	21 Neil Swanepoel*
22 Ignacio Corleto	22 Vincent Dreyer*
Referee Nigel Williams	

14 18/10/2003 — Suncorp Stadium

Australia: 90	Romania: 8
Tries: Flatley, Rogers (3), Burke (2), Larkham (2), Mortlock, Roff, Giteau, Tuqiri, Smith	Tries: Toderasc
Cons: Flatley (11)	Pens: Tofan
Pens: Flatley	
15 Mat Rogers	15 Danut Dumbrava
14 Wendell Sailor	14 Gabriel Brezoianu
13 Matt Burke	13 Valentin Maftei
12 Elton Flatley	12 Romeo Gontineac
11 Joe Roff	11 Cristian Sauan
10 Stephen Larkham	10 Ionut Tofan
9 George Gregan	9 Lucian Sirbu
1 Bill Young	1 Petrisor Toderasc
2 Brendan Cannon	2 Razvan Mavrodin
3 Al Baxter	3 Silviu Florea
4 Daniel Vickerman	4 Sorin Socol
5 Nathan Sharpe	5 Cristian Petre
6 George Smith	6 Marius Niculai
7 Phil Waugh	7 Ovidiu Tonita
8 David Lyons	8 George Chiriac
16 Jeremy Paul*	16 Cezar Popescu*
17 Ben Darwin*	17 Marcel Socaciu*
18 Justin Harrison*	18 Marian Tudori*
19 Matt Cockbain*	19 Bogdan Tudor*
20 Matt Giteau*	20 Cristian Podea*
21 Stirling Mortlock*	21 Mihai Vioreanu*
22 Lote Tuqiri*	22 Ioan Teodorescu*
Referee Pablo Deluca	

18 19/10/2003 — Aussie Stadium

Ireland 64	Namibia 7
Tries: Quinlan (2), Miller (2), Horan, Hickie, Dempsey, Horgan, G. Easterby, Kelly	Tries: Powell
Cons: O'Gara (7)	Cons: Wessels
15 Girvan Dempsey	15 Ronaldo Pedro
14 Shane Horgan	14 Deon Mouton
13 Brian O'Driscoll	13 Du Preez Grobler
12 Kevin Maggs	12 Corne Powell
11 Denis Hickie	11 Vincent Dreyer
10 Ronan O'Gara	10 Emile Wessels
9 Peter Stringer	9 Hakkies Husselman
1 Marcus Horan	1 Kees Lensing
2 Keith Wood	2 Johannes Meyer
3 John Hayes	3 Neil du Toit
4 Malcolm O'Kelly	4 Heino Senekal
5 Paul O'Connell	5 Archie Graham
6 Simon Easterby	6 Schalk van der Merwe
7 Alan Quinlan	7 Wolfie Duvenhage
8 Eric Miller	8 Sean Furter
16 Shane Byrne*	16 Cor Van Tonder*
17 Simon Best*	17 Andries Blaauw*
18 Donncha O'Callaghan	18 Herman Lintvelt*
19 Victor Costello	19 Jurgens van Lill*
20 Guy Easterby*	20 Neil Swanepoel*
21 David Humphreys	21 Melrick Africa*
22 John Kelly*	22 Morne Schreuder*
Referee Andrew Cole	

22 22/10/2003 — Aussie Stadium

Argentina 50	Romania 3
Tries: Gaitan, Hernandez (2), N. Fernandez Miranda, Bouza (2), Contepomi	Pens: Tofan
Cons: J. Fernandez Miranda (4), Quesada (2)	
Pens: J. Fernandez Miranda	
15 Juan Hernandez	15 Gabriel Brezoianu
14 J. M. Nunez Piossek	14 Mihai Vioreanu
13 Martin Gaitan	13 Valentin Maftei
12 Manuel Contepomi	12 Romeo Gontineac
11 Hernan Senillosa	11 Ioan Teodorescu
10 J. Fernandez Miranda	10 Ionut Tofan
9 N. Fernandez Miranda	9 Lucian Sirbu
1 Rodrigo Roncero	1 Petrisor Toderasc
2 Mario Ledesma	2 Razvan Mavrodin
3 Martin Scelzo	3 Silviu Florea
4 Pedro Sporleder	4 Sorin Socol
5 Patricio Albacete	5 Cristian Petre
6 Santiago Phelan	6 Marian Tudori
7 Martin Durand	7 Ovidiu Tonita
8 Pablo Bouza	8 George Chiriac
16 Federico Mendez	16 Ion Paulica*
17 Omar Hasan*	17 Cezar Popescu*
18 Rimas Alvarez	18 Augustin Petrichei*
19 Rolando Martin*	19 Vasile Ghioc*
20 Agustin Pichot*	20 Florin Tatu*
21 Gonzalo Quesada*	21 Iulian Andrei*
22 Jose Orengo	22 Cristian Sauan*
Referee Chris White	

26 25/10/2003 — Adelaide Oval

Australia 142	Namibia 0
Tries: Latham (5), Tuqiri (3), Giteau (3), Rogers (2), Turinui (2), Lyons, Mortlock, Paul, Grey, Burke, Roe, pen try	
Cons: Rogers (16)	
15 Chris Latham	15 Ronaldo Pedro
14 Lote Tuqiri	14 Deon Mouton
13 Stirling Mortlock	13 Du Preez Grobler
12 Nathan Grey	12 Emile Wessels
11 Mat Rogers	11 Jurie Booysen
10 Matt Giteau	10 Morne Schreuder
9 Chris Whitaker	9 Hakkies Husselman
1 Matt Dunning	1 Kees Lensing
2 Jeremy Paul	2 Cor Van Tonder
3 Ben Darwin	3 Neil du Toit
4 Justin Harrison	4 Heino Senekal
5 Nathan Sharpe	5 Eben Isaacs
6 George Smith	6 Shaun van Rooi
7 David Croft	7 Herman Lintvelt
8 David Lyons	8 Jurgens van Lill
16 Brendan Cannon	16 Phillipus Isaacs*
17 Bill Young	17 Andries Blaauw*
18 David Giffin*	18 Schalk van der Merwe*
19 John Roe*	19 Sean Furter*
20 Matt Cockbain*	20 Neil Swanepoel*
21 Morgan Turinui*	21 Deon Grunschloss*
22 Matt Burke*	22 Melrick Africa*
Referee Joel Jutge	

29 26/10/2003 — Adelaide Oval

Argentina: 15	Ireland: 16
Pens: Quesada (3)	Tries: Quinlan
DG: Quesada, Corleto	Cons: Humphreys
	Pens: Humphreys, O'Gara (2)
15 Ignacio Corleto	15 Girvan Dempsey
14 J. M. Nunez Piossek	14 Shane Horgan
13 Jose Orengo	13 Brian O'Driscoll
12 Felipe Contepomi	12 Kevin Maggs
11 Diego Albanese	11 Denis Hickie
10 Gonzalo Quesada	10 David Humphreys
9 Agustin Pichot	9 Peter Stringer
1 Roberto Grau	1 Reggie Corrigan
2 Federico Mendez	2 Keith Wood
3 Mauricio Reggiardo	3 John Hayes
4 I. Fernandez Lobbe	4 Malcolm O'Kelly
5 Rimas Alvarez	5 Paul O'Connell
6 Lucas Ostiglia	6 Simon Easterby
7 Rolando Martin	7 Alan Quinlan
8 Gonzalo Longo	8 Victor Costello
16 Mario Ledesma	16 Shane Byrne
17 Martin Scelzo	17 Marcus Horan*
18 Patricio Albacete	18 Donncha O'Callaghan
19 Santiago Phelan	19 Eric Miller*
20 N. Fernandez Miranda	20 Guy Easterby
21 Martin Gaitan	21 Ronan O'Gara*
22 Juan Hernandez	22 John Kelly
Referee Andre Watson	

34 30/10/2003 — York Park

Namibia 7	Romania 37
Tries: Isaacs	Tries: Petrichei, Chiriac, Sirbu, Teodorescu, Sauan
Cons: Wessels	Cons: Tofan (3)
	Pens: Tofan (2)
15 Ronaldo Pedro	15 Danut Dumbrava
14 Deon Mouton	14 Ioan Teodorescu
13 Du Preez Grobler	13 Valentin Maftei
12 Emile Wessels	12 Romeo Gontineac
11 Vincent Dreyer	11 Gabriel Brezoianu
10 Morne Schreuder	10 Ionut Tofan
9 Neil Swanepoel	9 Lucian Sirbu
1 Kees Lensing	1 Petru Balan
2 Johannes Meyer	2 Razvan Mavrodin
3 Neil du Toit	3 Marcel Socaciu
4 Heino Senekal	4 Augustin Petrichei
5 Eben Isaacs	5 Cristian Petre
6 Schalk van der Merwe	6 George Chiriac
7 Wolfie Duvenhage	7 Ovidiu Tonita
8 Sean Furter	8 Sorin Socol
16 Cor Van Tonder*	16 Cezar Popescu*
17 Andries Blaauw*	17 Petrisor Toderasc*
18 Herman Lintvelt	18 Silviu Florea*
19 Jurgens van Lill*	19 Marian Tudori*
20 Rudi van Vuuren	20 Iulian Andrei*
21 Deon Grunschloss*	21 Cristian Sauan*
22 Corne Powell*	22 Mihai Vioreanu*
Referee Peter Marshall	

38 1/11/2003 — Telstra Dome

Australia 17	Ireland 16
Tries: Smith	Tries: O'Driscoll
Pens: Flatley (3)	Cons: O'Gara
DG: Gregan	Pens: O'Gara (2)
	DG: O'Driscoll
15 Mat Rogers	15 Girvan Dempsey
14 Wendell Sailor	14 Shane Horgan
13 Matt Burke	13 Brian O'Driscoll
12 Elton Flatley	12 Kevin Maggs
11 Joe Roff	11 Denis Hickie
10 Stephen Larkham	10 Ronan O'Gara
9 George Gregan	9 Peter Stringer
1 Bill Young	1 Reggie Corrigan
2 Brendan Cannon	2 Keith Wood
3 Ben Darwin	3 John Hayes
4 David Giffin	4 Malcolm O'Kelly
5 Nathan Sharpe	5 Paul O'Connell
6 George Smith	6 Simon Easterby
7 Phil Waugh	7 Keith Gleeson
8 David Lyons	8 Anthony Foley
16 Jeremy Paul*	16 Shane Byrne
17 Al Baxter*	17 Marcus Horan*
18 Daniel Vickerman*	18 Donncha O'Callaghan*
19 Matt Cockbain*	19 Eric Miller*
20 Chris Whitaker	20 Guy Easterby
21 Matt Giteau*	21 David Humphreys*
22 Lote Tuqiri*	22 John Kelly*
Referee Paddy O'Brien	

FINAL POOL TABLE

	W	D	L	F	A	BP	PTS
Australia	4	0	0	273	32	2	18
Ireland	3	0	1	141	56	3	15
Argentina	2	0	2	140	57	3	11
Romania	1	0	3	65	192	1	5
Namibia	0	0	4	28	310	0	0

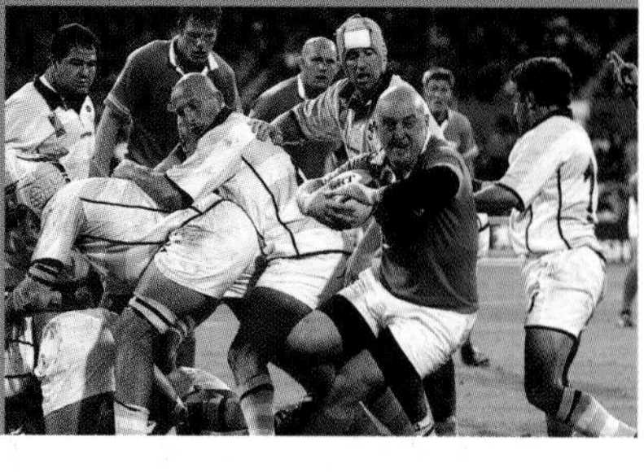

Pool B

4 11/10/2003 — Suncorp Stadium

France 61
Tries: Jauzion (3), Dominici (2), Ibanez, Harinordoquy
Cons: Michalak (4)
Pens: Michalak (6)

15 Nicolas Brusque
14 Aurelien Rougerie
13 Tony Marsh
12 Yannick Jauzion
11 Christophe Dominici
10 Frederic Michalak
9 Fabien Galthie
1 Jean Jacques Crenca
2 Raphael Ibanez
3 Jean Baptiste Poux
4 Fabien Pelous
5 Jerome Thion
6 Serge Betsen
7 Olivier Magne
8 Imanol Harinordoquy

16 Yannick Bru
17 Olivier Milloud
18 Olivier Brouzet*
19 Christian Labit*
20 Gerald Merceron*
21 Damien Traille*
22 Pepito Elhorga*

Fiji 18
Tries: Caucau, Naevo
Cons: Little
Pens: Little (2)

15 Norman Ligairi
14 Vilimoni Delasau
13 Aisea Tuilevu
12 Seru Rabeni
11 Rupeni Caucau
10 Nicky Little
9 Moses Rauluni
1 Richard Nyholt
2 Greg Smith
3 Joeli Veitayaki
4 Ifereimi Rawaqa
5 Api Naevo
6 Sisa Koyamaibole
7 Kitione Salawa
8 Alifereti Doviverata

16 Bill Gadolo
17 Nacanieli Seru*
18 Kele Leawere*
19 Koli Sewabu*
20 Sami Rabaka*
21 Waisale Serevi*
22 Marika Vunibaka*

Referee Alain Rolland

7 12/10/2003 — Dairy Farmers Sdm

Scotland: 32
Tries: Paterson (2), Grimes, Taylor, Danielli
Cons: Paterson, Townsend
Pens: Paterson

15 Ben Hinshelwood
14 Chris Paterson
13 Andy Craig
12 James McLaren
11 Kenny Logan
10 Gordon Ross
9 Bryan Redpath
1 Tom Smith
2 Rob Russell
3 Bruce Douglas
4 Scott Murray
5 Stuart Grimes
6 Jason White
7 Jon Petrie
8 Simon Taylor

16 Gordon Bulloch
17 Gavin Kerr*
18 Ross Beattie*
19 Martin Leslie*
20 Michael Blair
21 Gregor Townsend*
22 Simon Danielli*

Japan: 11
Tries: Onozawa
Pens: Hirose (2)

15 Tsutomu Matsuda
14 Daisuke Ohata
13 Ruben Parkinson
12 Yukio Motoki
11 Hirotoki Onozawa
10 Keiji Hirose
9 Takashi Tsuji
1 Shin Hasegawa
2 Masao Amino
3 Masahiko Toyoyama
4 Hajime Kiso
5 Adam Parker
6 Naoya Okubo
7 Takuro Miuchi
8 Takeomi Ito

16 Masahito Yamamoto
17 Masaaki Sakata*
18 Hiroyuki Tanuma
19 Yasunori Watanabe*
20 Yuji Sonoda*
21 Andrew Miller*
22 Toru Kurihara*

Referee Stuart Dickinson

10 15/10/2003 — Suncorp Stadium

Fiji: 19
Tries: Naevo
Cons: Little
Pens: Little (4)

15 Alfred Uluinayau
14 Marika Vunibaka
13 Aisea Tuilevu
12 Seru Rabeni
11 Vilimoni Delasau
10 Nicky Little
9 Moses Rauluni
1 Joeli Veitayaki
2 Greg Smith
3 Nacanieli Seru
4 Ifereimi Rawaqa
5 Api Naevo
6 Alivereti Mocelutu
7 Koli Sewabu
8 Alifereti Doviverata

16 Bill Gadolo
17 Richard Nyholt*
18 Vula Maimuri*
19 Sisa Koyamaibole*
20 Waisale Serevi
21 Epeli Ruivadra
22 Norman Ligairi

USA: 18
Tries: van Zyl, Schubert
Cons: Hercus
Pens: Hercus (2)

15 Paul Emerick
14 David Fee
13 Phillip Eloff
12 Kain Cross
11 Riaan van Zyl
10 Mike Hercus
9 Kevin Dalzell
1 Mike MacDonald
2 Kirk Khasigian
3 Daniel Dorsey
4 Alec Parker
5 Luke Gross
6 Kort Schubert
7 Dave Hodges
8 Dan Lyle

16 Matthew Wyatt
17 John Tarpoff
18 Gerhard Klerck
19 Jurie Gouws
20 Kimball Kjar
21 Salesi Sika*
22 John Buchholz*

Referee Joel Jutge

15 18/10/2003 — Dairy Farmers Sdm

France: 51
Tries: Rougerie (2), Michalak, Pelous, Dominici, Crenca
Cons: Michalak (5), Merceron
Pens: Michalak (3)

15 Clement Poitrenaud
14 Aurelien Rougerie
13 Tony Marsh
12 Damien Traille
11 Christophe Dominici
10 Frederic Michalak
9 Fabien Galthie
1 Olivier Milloud
2 Yannick Bru
3 Jean Baptiste Poux
4 Fabien Pelous
5 Olivier Brouzet
6 Serge Betsen
7 Olivier Magne
8 Christian Labit

16 Raphael Ibanez*
17 Jean Jacques Crenca*
18 David Auradou*
19 Sebastien Chabal*
20 Gerald Merceron*
21 Yannick Jauzion
22 Pepito Elhorga

Japan: 29
Tries: Konia, Ohata
Cons: Kurihara (2)
Pens: Kurihara (5)

15 Toru Kurihara
14 Daisuke Ohata
13 George Konia
12 Hideki Namba
11 Hirotoki Onozawa
10 Andrew Miller
9 Yuji Sonoda
1 Shin Hasegawa
2 Masaaki Sakata
3 Ryo Yamamura
4 Hiroyuki Tanuma
5 Adam Parker
6 Naoya Okubo
7 Takuro Miuchi
8 Takeomi Ito

16 Masahito Yamamoto
17 Masao Amino
18 Koichi Kubo*
19 Ryota Asano*
20 Takashi Tsuji
21 Yukio Motoki
22 Takashi Yoshida

Referee Alan Lewis

20 20/10/2003 — Suncorp Stadium

Scotland 39
Tries: Danielli (2), Kerr, Townsend, Paterson
Cons: Paterson (4)
Pens: Paterson (2)

15 Glenn Metcalfe
14 Simon Danielli
13 Andy Craig
12 Andrew Henderson
11 Chris Paterson
10 Gregor Townsend
9 Michael Blair
1 Tom Smith
2 Gordon Bulloch
3 Gavin Kerr
4 Nathan Hines
5 Stuart Grimes
6 Ross Beattie
7 Jon Petrie
8 Simon Taylor

16 Rob Russell
17 Bruce Douglas*
18 Jason White*
19 Martin Leslie*
20 Bryan Redpath*
21 Ben Hinshelwood*
22 Kenny Logan*

USA 15
Pens: Hercus (5)

15 Paul Emerick
14 David Fee
13 Phillip Eloff
12 Kain Cross
11 Riaan van Zyl
10 Mike Hercus
9 Kevin Dalzell
1 Mike MacDonald
2 Kirk Khasigian
3 Daniel Dorsey
4 Alec Parker
5 Luke Gross
6 Kort Schubert
7 Dave Hodges
8 Dan Lyle

16 Matthew Wyatt
17 Richard Liddington*
18 Jurie Gouws*
19 Oloseti Fifita*
20 Kimball Kjar*
21 Jason Keyter*
22 Link Wilfley*

Referee Jonathan Kaplan

23 23/10/2003 — Dairy Farmers Sdm

Fiji 41
Tries: Ligairi (2), Tuilevu (2), Vunibaka
Cons: Little (2)
Pens: Little (3), Serevi

15 Norman Ligairi
14 Aisea Tuilevu
13 Epeli Ruivadra
12 Seru Rabeni
11 Vilimoni Delasau
10 Waisale Serevi
9 Sami Rabaka
1 Isaia Rasila
2 Greg Smith
3 Nacanieli Seru
4 Emori Katalau
5 Kele Leawere
6 Alivereti Mocelutu
7 Koli Sewabu
8 Alifereti Doviverata

16 Bill Gadolo*
17 Joeli Veitayaki*
18 Sisa Koyamaibole*
19 Vula Maimuri*
20 Moses Rauluni*
21 Nicky Little*
22 Marika Vunibaka*

Japan 13
Tries: Miller
Cons: Miller
Pens: Miller
DG: Miller

15 Tsutomu Matsuda
14 Daisuke Ohata
13 Ruben Parkinson
12 Yukio Motoki
11 Hirotoki Onozawa
10 Andrew Miller
9 Takashi Tsuji
1 Masahito Yamamoto
2 Masaaki Sakata
3 Masahiko Toyoyama
4 Hajime Kiso
5 Adam Parker
6 Naoya Okubo
7 Takuro Miuchi
8 Takeomi Ito

16 Shin Hasegawa*
17 Masao Amino*
18 Koichi Kubo*
19 Ryota Asano*
20 Yuji Sonoda*
21 George Konia*
22 Toru Kurihara*

Referee Nigel Williams

28 25/10/2003 — Telstra Stadium

France 51
Tries: Betsen, Harinordoquy, Michalak, Galthie, Brusque
Cons: Michalak (4)
Pens: Michalak (4)
DG: Michalak, Brusque

15 Nicolas Brusque
14 Aurelien Rougerie
13 Tony Marsh
12 Yannick Jauzion
11 Christophe Dominici
10 Frederic Michalak
9 Fabien Galthie
1 Jean Jacques Crenca
2 Raphael Ibanez
3 Sylvain Marconnet
4 Fabien Pelous
5 Jerome Thion
6 Serge Betsen
7 Olivier Magne
8 Imanol Harinordoquy

16 Yannick Bru*
17 Olivier Milloud*
18 Olivier Brouzet*
19 Patrick Tabacco*
20 Gerald Merceron*
21 Damien Traille*
22 Pepito Elhorga

Scotland 9
Pens: Paterson (3)

15 Glenn Metcalfe
14 Chris Paterson
13 Andy Craig
12 Andrew Henderson
11 Kenny Logan
10 Gregor Townsend
9 Bryan Redpath
1 Tom Smith
2 Gordon Bulloch
3 Gavin Kerr
4 Scott Murray
5 Stuart Grimes
6 Jason White
7 Cameron Mather
8 Simon Taylor

16 Rob Russell*
17 Bruce Douglas*
18 Nathan Hines*
19 Jon Petrie*
20 Michael Blair
21 James McLaren*
22 Simon Danielli

Referee David McHugh

31 27/10/2003 — Central Coast Sdm

Japan: 26
Tries: Kurihara, Ohata
Cons: Kurihara (2)
Pens: Kurihara (4)

15 Tsutomu Matsuda
14 Daisuke Ohata
13 George Konia
12 Yukio Motoki
11 Toru Kurihara
10 Andrew Miller
9 Yuji Sonoda
1 Shin Hasegawa
2 Masao Amino
3 Masahiko Toyoyama
4 Hajime Kiso
5 Adam Parker
6 Naoya Okubo
7 Takuro Miuchi
8 Takeomi Ito

16 Masahito Yamamoto*
17 Masaaki Sakata
18 Koichi Kubo
19 Yuya Saito*
20 Takashi Tsuji*
21 Hideki Namba
22 Hirotoki Onozawa*

USA: 39
Tries: Hercus, Eloff, Schubert, van Zyl, Khasigian
Cons: Hercus (4)
Pens: Hercus (2)

15 Paul Emerick
14 David Fee
13 Phillip Eloff
12 Salesi Sika
11 Riaan van Zyl
10 Mike Hercus
9 Kevin Dalzell
1 Mike MacDonald
2 Kirk Khasigian
3 Daniel Dorsey
4 Gerhard Klerck
5 Luke Gross
6 Kort Schubert
7 Dave Hodges
8 Dan Lyle

16 Matthew Wyatt*
17 Jacob Waasdorp*
18 Jurie Gouws
19 Oloseti Fifita
20 Kimball Kjar*
21 Jason Keyter
22 John Buchholz*

Referee Steve Walsh

35 31/10/2003 — WIN Stadium

France 41
Tries: Liebenberg (3), Poux, Bru
Cons: Merceron (2)
Pens: Merceron (3)
DG: Yachvili

15 Clement Poitrenaud
14 Pepito Elhorga
13 Brian Liebenberg
12 Damien Traille
11 David Bory
10 Gerald Merceron
9 Dmitri Yachvili
1 Olivier Milloud
2 Yannick Bru
3 Jean Baptiste Poux
4 David Auradou
5 Olivier Brouzet
6 Sebastien Chabal
7 Patrick Tabacco
8 Christian Labit

16 Raphael Ibanez
17 Sylvain Marconnet*
18 Jerome Thion
19 Olivier Magne
20 Frederic Michalak
21 Yannick Jauzion
22 Aurelien Rougerie

USA 14
Tries: Schubert, Hercus
Cons: Hercus (2)

15 John Buchholz
14 David Fee
13 Phillip Eloff
12 Salesi Sika
11 Riaan van Zyl
10 Mike Hercus
9 Kevin Dalzell
1 Mike MacDonald
2 Kirk Khasigian
3 Daniel Dorsey
4 Alec Parker
5 Luke Gross
6 Kort Schubert
7 Dave Hodges
8 Dan Lyle

16 Matthew Wyatt*
17 Jacob Waasdorp*
18 Gerhard Klerck
19 Jurie Gouws*
20 Matt Sherman*
21 Jason Keyter*
22 Mose Timoteo*

Referee Paul Honiss

36 1/11/2003 — Aussie Stadium

Scotland 22
Tries: Smith
Cons: Paterson
Pens: Paterson (5)

15 Glenn Metcalfe
14 Simon Danielli
13 Gregor Townsend
12 Andrew Henderson
11 Kenny Logan
10 Chris Paterson
9 Bryan Redpath
1 Tom Smith
2 Gordon Bulloch
3 Bruce Douglas
4 Nathan Hines
5 Stuart Grimes
6 Ross Beattie
7 Cameron Mather
8 Simon Taylor

16 Rob Russell*
17 Gordon McIlwham
18 Jason White*
19 Jon Petrie
20 Michael Blair
21 James McLaren*
22 Ben Hinshelwood*

Fiji 20
Tries: Caucau (2)
Cons: Little (2)
Pens: Little (2)

15 Norman Ligairi
14 Aisea Tuilevu
13 Epeli Ruivadra
12 Seru Rabeni
11 Rupeni Caucau
10 Nicky Little
9 Moses Rauluni
1 Isaia Rasila
2 Greg Smith
3 Joeli Veitayaki
4 Ifereimi Rawaqa
5 Api Naevo
6 Vula Maimuri
7 Koli Sewabu
8 Alifereti Doviverata

16 Nacanieli Seru*
17 Setareki Tawake
18 Sisa Koyamaibole*
19 Kitione Salawa*
20 Jacob Rauluni*
21 Isikeli Nacewa*
22 Vilimoni Delasau*

Referee Tony Spreadbury

FINAL POOL TABLE

	W	D	L	F	A	BP	PTS
France	4	0	0	204	70	4	20
Scotland	3	0	1	102	97	2	14
Fiji	2	0	2	98	114	2	10
USA	1	0	3	86	125	2	6
Japan	0	0	4	79	163	0	0

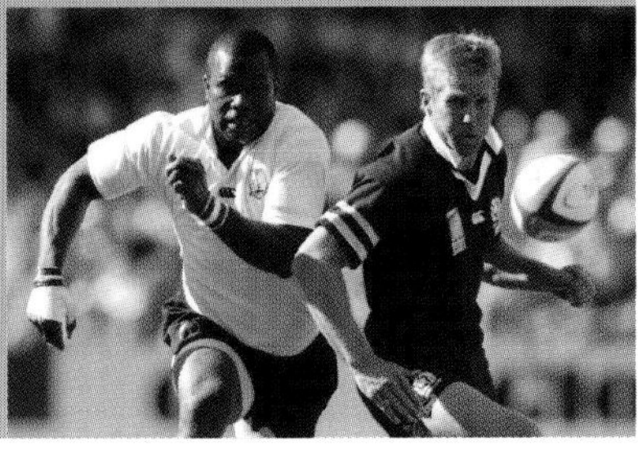

Pool C

5 11/10/2003 — Subiaco Oval

South Africa 72
Tries: vd Westhuizen (3), Botha (2), Van Niekerk, Fourie, Bands, Delport, Rossouw, Scholtz, Greeff
Cons: Koen (5), Hougaard

Uruguay 6
Pens: D. Aguirre (2)

South Africa	Uruguay
15 Werner Greeff	15 Joaquin Pastore
14 Ashwin Willemse	14 Alfonso Cardoso
13 Jaque Fourie	13 Diego Aguirre
12 De Wet Barry	12 Martin Mendaro
11 Thinus Delport	11 Emiliano Ibarra
10 Louis Koen	10 Sebastian Aguirre
9 Joost vd Westhuizen	9 Emiliano Caffera
1 Lawrence Sephaka	1 Rodrigo Sanchez
2 Danie Coetzee	2 Diego Lamelas
3 Richard Bands	3 Pablo Lemoine
4 Bakkies Botha	4 Juan Carlos Bado
5 Victor Matfield	5 Juan Alzueta
6 Joe Van Niekerk	6 Nicolas Brignoni
7 Danie Rossouw	7 Marcelo Gutierrez
8 Juan Smith	8 Rodrigo Capo
16 John Smit*	16 Juan Andres Perez*
17 Faan Rautenbach*	17 Eduardo Berruti*
18 Selborne Boome*	18 Guillermo Storace*
19 Hendro Scholtz*	19 Nicolas Grille*
20 Neil de Kock*	20 Hernan Ponte*
21 Derick Hougaard*	21 Bernardo Amarillo*
22 Ricardo Loubscher*	22 Juan Menchaca*

Referee Paddy O'Brien

8 12/10/2003 — Subiaco Oval

England: 84
Tries: Cohen (2), Greenwood (2), Tindall, Dawson, Regan, Thompson, Back, Dallaglio, Robinson, Luger
Cons: Wilkinson (5), Grayson (4)
Pens: Wilkinson (2)

Georgia: 6
Pens: Urjukashvili, Jimsheladze

England	Georgia
15 Josh Lewsey	15 Besik Khamashuridze
14 Jason Robinson	14 Malkhaz Urjukashvili
13 Will Greenwood	13 Tedo Zibzibadze
12 Mike Tindall	12 Irakli Giorgadze
11 Ben Cohen	11 Vasil Katsadze
10 Jonny Wilkinson	10 Paliko Jimsheladze
9 Matt Dawson	9 Irakli Abuseridze
1 Trevor Woodman	1 Goderdzi Shvelidze
2 Steve Thompson	2 Akvsenti Giorgadze
3 Phil Vickery	3 A. Margvelashvili
4 Martin Johnson	4 Zurab Mchedlishvili
5 Ben Kay	5 Victor Didebulidze
6 Richard Hill	6 Gia Labadze
7 Neil Back	7 Gregoire Yachvili
8 Lawrence Dallaglio	8 George Chkhaidze
16 Mark Regan*	16 David Dadunashvili*
17 Jason Leonard*	17 Soso Nikolaenko*
18 Danny Grewcock	18 Vano Nadiradze*
19 Lewis Moody*	19 David Bolgashvili*
20 Andy Gomarsall*	20 Merab Kvirikashvili*
21 Paul Grayson*	21 Irakli Machkhaneli*
22 Dan Luger*	22 Badri Khekhelashvili*

Referee Pablo Deluca

12 15/10/2003 — Subiaco Oval

Samoa: 60
Tries: Fa'asavalu (2), Lima (2), Tagicakibau, Fa'atau, Lemalu, Vili, Feaunati, Palepoi
Cons: Va'a (3), Vili (2)

Uruguay: 13
Tries: Capo, Lemoine
Pens: Aguirre

Samoa	Uruguay
15 Tanner Vili	15 Juan Menchaca
14 Lome Fa'atau	14 Joaquin Pastore
13 Terry Fanolua	13 Diego Aguirre
12 Brian Lima	12 Martin Mendaro
11 Sailosi Tagicakibau	11 Carlos Baldasarri
10 Earl Va'a	10 Bernardo Amarillo
9 Steven So'oialo	9 Juan Campomar
1 Kas Lealamanu'a	1 Rodrigo Sanchez
2 Jonathan Meredith	2 Diego Lamelas
3 Jeremy Tomuli	3 Pablo Lemoine
4 Opeta Palepoi	4 Juan Carlos Bado
5 Leo Lafaiali'I	5 Juan Alzueta
6 Peter Poulos	6 Marcelo Gutierrez
7 Maurie Fa'asavalu	7 Nicolas Grille
8 Semo Sititi	8 Rodrigo Capo
16 Mahonri Schwalger*	16 Juan Andres Perez*
17 Simon Lemalu*	17 Juan Machado*
18 Kitiona Viliamu*	18 Juan Miguel Alvarez*
19 Des Tuiavi'I*	19 Nicolas Brignoni*
20 Denning Tyrell*	20 Ignacio Conti*
21 Dale Rasmussen*	21 Joaquin De Freitas*
22 Dominic Feaunati*	22 Jose Viana*

Referee David McHugh

16 18/10/2003 — Subiaco Oval

South Africa: 6
Pens: Koen (2)

England: 25
Tries: Greenwood
Cons: Wilkinson
Pens: Wilkinson (4)
DG: Wilkinson (2)

South Africa	England
15 Jaco vd Westhuyzen	15 Josh Lewsey
14 Ashwin Willemse	14 Jason Robinson
13 Jorrie Muller	13 Will Greenwood
12 De Wet Barry	12 Mike Tindall
11 Thinus Delport	11 Ben Cohen
10 Louis Koen	10 Jonny Wilkinson
9 Joost vd Westhuizen	9 Kyran Bracken
1 Christo Bezuidenhout	1 Trevor Woodman
2 Danie Coetzee	2 Steve Thompson
3 Richard Bands	3 Phil Vickery
4 Bakkies Botha	4 Martin Johnson
5 Victor Matfield	5 Ben Kay
6 Corne Krige	6 Lewis Moody
7 Joe Van Niekerk	7 Neil Back
8 Juan Smith	8 Lawrence Dallaglio
16 John Smit*	16 Dorian West
17 Lawrence Sephaka*	17 Jason Leonard*
18 Selborne Boome	18 Martin Corry
19 Danie Rossouw	19 Joe Worsley*
20 Neil de Kock	20 Andy Gomarsall
21 Derick Hougaard*	21 Paul Grayson
22 Werner Greeff	22 Dan Luger*

Referee Peter Marshall

19 19/10/2003 — Subiaco Oval

Samoa 46
Tries: Tagicakibau, Va'a, So'oialo, Sititi, Lima, Feaunati
Cons: Va'a (5)
Pens: Va'a (2)

Georgia 9
Pens: Jimsheladze (2)
DG: Jimsheladze

Samoa	Georgia
15 Tanner Vili	15 Badri Khekhelashvili
14 Ron Fanuatanu	14 Malkhaz Urjukashvili
13 Terry Fanolua	13 Tedo Zibzibadze
12 Brian Lima	12 Irakli Giorgadze
11 Sailosi Tagicakibau	11 Vasil Katsadze
10 Earl Va'a	10 Paliko Jimsheladze
9 Steven So'oialo	9 Irakli Abuseridze
1 Kas Lealamanu'a	1 Goderdzi Shvelidze
2 Jonathan Meredith	2 Akvsenti Giorgadze
3 Jeremy Tomuli	3 Soso Nikolaenko
4 Opeta Palepoi	4 Zurab Mchedlishvili
5 Leo Lafaiali'I	5 Vano Nadiradze
6 Peter Poulos	6 Gia Labadze
7 Maurie Fa'asavalu	7 Gregoire Yachvili
8 Semo Sititi	8 Ilia Zedginidze
16 Mahonri Schwalger*	16 David Dadunashvili
17 Simon Lemalu*	17 A. Margvelashvili*
18 Kitiona Viliamu*	18 Victor Didebulidze*
19 Siaosi Vaili*	19 David Bolgashvili*
20 Denning Tyrell*	20 Merab Kvirikashvili*
21 Dale Rasmussen*	21 Irakli Machkhaneli*
22 Dominic Feaunati*	22 Besik Khamashuridze*

Referee Alain Rolland

25 24/10/2003 — Aussie Stadium

South Africa 46
Tries: Rossouw (2), Van Niekerk, Fourie, Botha, Burger, Hougaard
Cons: Hougaard (4)
Pens: Hougaard

Georgia 19
Tries: Dadunashvilli
Cons: Jimsheladze
Pens: Jimsheladze (3), Kvirikashvili

South Africa	Georgia
15 Ricardo Loubscher	15 Irakli Machkhaneli
14 Stefan Terblanche	14 Gocha Khonelidze
13 Jaque Fourie	13 Otar Eloshvili
12 Werner Greeff	12 Vasil Katsadze
11 Breyton Paulse	11 Archil Kavtarashvili
10 Derick Hougaard	10 Paliko Jimsheladze
9 Neil de Kock	9 Irakli Modebadze
1 Lawrence Sephaka	1 Avtandil Kopaliani
2 John Smit	2 David Dadunashvili
3 Faan Rautenbach	3 A. Margvelashvili
4 Bakkies Botha	4 Sergo Gujaraidze
5 Selborne Boome	5 Victor Didebulidze
6 Hendro Scholtz	6 George Tsiklauri
7 Danie Rossouw	7 David Bolgashvili
8 Joe Van Niekerk	8 George Chkhaidze
16 Dale Santon*	16 Akvsenti Giorgadze*
17 Christo Bezuidenhout	17 Soso Nikolaenko*
18 Victor Matfield	18 Ilia Zedginidze*
19 Schalk Burger*	19 Gregoire Yachvili
20 Joost vd Westhuizen	20 Irakli Abuseridze*
21 Louis Koen	21 Merab Kvirikashvili*
22 Jorrie Muller*	22 Besik Khamashuridze*

Referee Stuart Dickinson

30 26/10/2003 — Telstra Dome

England 35
Tries: Back, pen try, Balshaw, Vickery
Cons: Wilkinson (3)
Pens: Wilkinson (2)
DG: Wilkinson

Samoa 22
Tries: Sititi
Cons: Va'a
Pens: Va'a (5)

England	Samoa
15 Jason Robinson	15 Tanner Vili
14 Iain Balshaw	14 Lome Fa'atau
13 Stuart Abbott	13 Terry Fanolua
12 Mike Tindall	12 Brian Lima
11 Ben Cohen	11 Sailosi Tagicakibau
10 Jonny Wilkinson	10 Earl Va'a
9 Matt Dawson	9 Steven So'oialo
1 Jason Leonard	1 Kas Lealamanu'a
2 Mark Regan	2 Jonathan Meredith
3 Julian White	3 Jeremy Tomuli
4 Martin Johnson	4 Opeta Palepoi
5 Ben Kay	5 Leo Lafaiali'I
6 Joe Worsley	6 Peter Poulos
7 Neil Back	7 Maurie Fa'asavalu
8 Lawrence Dallaglio	8 Semo Sititi
16 Steve Thompson*	16 Mahonri Schwalger*
17 Phil Vickery*	17 Simon Lemalu*
18 Martin Corry	18 Kitiona Viliamu*
19 Lewis Moody*	19 Des Tuiavi'I*
20 Andy Gomarsall	20 Denning Tyrell*
21 Mike Catt*	21 Dale Rasmussen*
22 Dan Luger	22 Dominic Feaunati*

Referee Jonathan Kaplan

32 28/10/2003 — Aussie Stadium

Uruguay 24
Tries: Cardoso, Lamelas, Brignoni
Cons: D. Aguirre (2), Menchaca
Pens: Menchaca

Georgia: 12
Pens: Urjukashvili, Kvirikashvili (3)

Uruguay	Georgia
15 Juan Menchaca	15 Irakli Machkhaneli
14 Alfonso Cardoso	14 Malkhaz Urjukashvili
13 Diego Aguirre	13 Tedo Zibzibadze
12 Martin Mendaro	12 Irakli Giorgadze
11 Carlos Baldasarri	11 Archil Kavtarashvili
10 Sebastian Aguirre	10 Paliko Jimsheladze
9 Juan Campomar	9 Irakli Modebadze
1 Rodrigo Sanchez	1 Goderdzi Shvelidze
2 Diego Lamelas	2 David Dadunashvili
3 Pablo Lemoine	3 Avtandil Kopaliani
4 Juan Carlos Bado	4 Zurab Mchedlishvili
5 Juan Alzueta	5 Sergo Gujaraidze
6 Hernan Ponte	6 George Chkhaidze
7 Nicolas Grille	7 Gregoire Yachvili
8 Rodrigo Capo	8 Ilia Zedginidze
16 Juan Andres Perez*	16 Akvsenti Giorgadze*
17 Eduardo Berruti*	17 Soso Nikolaenko*
18 Guillermo Storace*	18 George Tsiklauri*
19 Nicolas Brignoni*	19 David Bolgashvili
20 Marcelo Gutierrez*	20 Merab Kvirikashvili*
21 Bernardo Amarillo*	21 Vasil Katsadze*
22 Joaquin Pastore*	22 Besik Khamashuridze*

Referee Kelvin Deaker

37 1/11/2003 — Suncorp Stadium

South Africa 60
Tries: Van Niekerk, Muller, Hougaard, Smith, Willemse, Fourie, van der Westhuyzen, de Kock
Cons: Hougaard (5), Koen (2)
Pens: Hougaard
DG: Hougaard

Samoa 10
Tries: Palepoi
Cons: Va'a
Pens: Va'a

South Africa	Samoa
15 Jaco vd Westhuyzen	15 Tanner Vili
14 Ashwin Willemse	14 Lome Fa'atau
13 Jorrie Muller	13 Romi Ropati
12 De Wet Barry	12 Brian Lima
11 Thinus Delport	11 Sailosi Tagicakibau
10 Derick Hougaard	10 Earl Va'a
9 Joost vd Westhuizen	9 Steven So'oialo
1 Christo Bezuidenhout	1 Kas Lealamanu'a
2 John Smit	2 Jonathan Meredith
3 Faan Rautenbach	3 Jeremy Tomuli
4 Bakkies Botha	4 Opeta Palepoi
5 Victor Matfield	5 Leo Lafaiali'I
6 Corne Krige	6 Peter Poulos
7 Joe Van Niekerk	7 Maurie Fa'asavalu
8 Juan Smith	8 Semo Sititi
16 Danie Coetzee*	16 Mahonri Schwalger
17 Richard Bands*	17 Tamato Leupolu*
18 Danie Rossouw*	18 Kitiona Viliamu*
19 Schalk Burger*	19 Des Tuiavi'I*
20 Neil de Kock*	20 Denning Tyrell*
21 Louis Koen*	21 Dale Rasmussen*
22 Jaque Fourie*	22 Dominic Feaunati*

Referee Chris White

39 2/11/2003 — Suncorp Stadium

England 111
Tries: Lewsey (5), Balshaw (2), Catt (2), Gomarsall (2), Robinson (2), Luger, Abbott, Greenwood, Moody.
Cons: Grayson (11), Catt (2)

Uruguay 13
Tries: Lemoine
Cons: Menchaca
Pens: Menchaca (2)

England	Uruguay
15 Josh Lewsey	15 Juan Menchaca
14 Iain Balshaw	14 Joaquin Pastore
13 Stuart Abbott	13 Diego Aguirre
12 Mike Catt	12 Joaquin De Freitas
11 Dan Luger	11 Jose Viana
10 Paul Grayson	10 Sebastian Aguirre
9 Andy Gomarsall	9 Juan Campomar
1 Jason Leonard	1 Eduardo Berruti
2 Dorian West	2 Diego Lamelas
3 Phil Vickery	3 Pablo Lemoine
4 Martin Corry	4 Juan Carlos Bado
5 Danny Grewcock	5 Juan Miguel Alvarez
6 Joe Worsley	6 Nicolas Brignoni
7 Lewis Moody	7 Nicolas Grille
8 Lawrence Dallaglio	8 Rodrigo Capo
16 Steve Thompson	16 Juan Andres Perez*
17 Julian White*	17 Rodrigo Sanchez*
18 Martin Johnson*	18 Guillermo Storace*
19 Ben Kay	19 Juan Alzueta*
20 Kyran Bracken*	20 Marcelo Gutierrez*
21 Will Greenwood*	21 Emiliano Caffera*
22 Jason Robinson*	22 Diego Reyes*

Referee Nigel Williams

FINAL POOL TABLE

	W	D	L	F	A	BP	PTS
England	4	0	0	255	47	3	19
South Africa	3	0	1	184	60	3	15
Samoa	2	0	2	138	117	2	10
Uruguay	1	0	3	56	255	0	4
Georgia	0	0	4	46	200	0	0

2 11/10/2003 — Telstra Dome

New Zealand: 70	Italy: 7
Tries: Thorn, Thorne, Howlett (2), Spencer (2), Rokocoko (2), Marshall, Carter, MacDonald	Tries: Phillips
Cons: Carter (6)	Cons: Peens
Pens: Spencer	
15 Mils Muliaina	15 Gert Peens
14 Doug Howlett	14 Mirco Bergamasco
13 Tana Umaga	13 Andrea Masi
12 Daniel Carter	12 Matteo Barbini
11 Joe Rokocoko	11 Nicola Mazzucato
10 Carlos Spencer	10 Francesco Mazzariol
9 Justin Marshall	9 Matteo Mazzantini
1 Dave Hewett	1 Salvatore Perugini
2 Keven Mealamu	2 Carlo Festuccia
3 Greg Somerville	3 Ramiro Martinez
4 Brad Thorn	4 Carlo Checchinato
5 Chris Jack	5 Christian Bezzi
6 Reuben Thorne	6 Scott Palmer
7 Richie McCaw	7 Mauro Bergamasco
8 Jerry Collins	8 Matthew Phillips
16 Mark Hammett*	16 Fabio Ongaro*
17 Kees Meeuws*	17 Martin Castrogiovanni*
18 Rodney So'oialo*	18 Sergio Parisse*
19 Marty Holah*	19 Andrea Benatti*
20 Steve Devine	20 Alessandro Troncon*
21 Ma'a Nonu*	21 Rima Wakarua
22 Leon MacDonald*	22 Gonzalo Canale*

Referee Andrew Cole

6 12/10/2003 — Telstra Dome

Wales 41	Canada 10
Tries: M. Jones, Parker, G. Thomas, Cooper, Charvis	Tries: Tkachuk
Cons: Harris (5)	Cons: Pritchard
Pens: Harris (2)	DG: Ross
15 Kevin Morgan	15 James Pritchard
14 Mark Jones	14 Winston Stanley
13 Sonny Parker	13 Nikyta Witkowski
12 Iestyn Harris	12 Marco di Girolamo
11 Gareth Thomas	11 Dave Lougheed
10 Ceri Sweeney	10 Bob Ross
9 Gareth Cooper	9 Morgan Williams
1 Duncan Jones	1 Rod Snow
2 Robin McBryde	2 Mark Lawson
3 Gethin Jenkins	3 Jon Thiel
4 Brent Cockbain	4 Colin Yukes
5 Gareth Llewellyn	5 Mike James
6 Dafydd Jones	6 Al Charron
7 Martyn Williams	7 Adam van Staveren
8 Colin Charvis	8 Josh Jackson
16 Huw Bennett*	16 Aaron Abrams
17 Adam Jones*	17 Kevin Tkachuk*
18 Robert Sidoli*	18 Garth Cooke*
19 Jonathan Thomas	19 Jamie Cudmore*
20 Dwayne Peel*	20 Ryan Banks
21 Mark Taylor*	21 Ed Fairhurst
22 Rhys Williams	22 Ryan Smith*

Referee Chris White

11 15/10/2003 — Canberra Sdm

Italy 36	Tonga 12
Tries: M. Dallan, D. Dallan (2)	Tries: Payne, Tu'ifua
Cons: Wakarua (3)	Cons: Tu'ipulotu
Pens: Wakarua (5)	
15 Gonzalo Canale	15 Pierre Hola
14 Nicola Mazzucato	14 Sione Fonua
13 Cristian Stoica	13 Gus Leger
12 Manuel Dallan	12 John Payne
11 Denis Dallan	11 Tevita Tu'ifua
10 Rima Wakarua	10 Sateki Tu'ipulotu
9 Alessandro Troncon	9 Sililo Martens
1 Andrea Lo Cicero	1 Tonga Lea'aetoa
2 Fabio Ongaro	2 Ephram Taukafa
3 Martin Castrogiovanni	3 Heamani Lavaka
4 Santiago Dellape	4 Milton Ngauamo
5 Marco Bortolami	5 Viliami Vaki
6 Andrea De Rossi	6 Inoke Afeaki
7 Aaron Persico	7 Ipolito Fenukitau
8 Sergio Parisse	8 Benhur Kivalu
16 Carlo Festuccia*	16 Viliami Ma'asi*
17 Salvatore Perugini*	17 Kisi Pulu*
18 Carlo Checchinato*	18 Usaia Latu*
19 Mauro Bergamasco*	19 Stanley Afeaki*
20 Matteo Mazzantini	20 Anthony Alatini
21 Francesco Mazzariol	21 Johnny Ngauamo*
22 Andrea Masi*	22 Sila Va'enuku*

Referee Steve Walsh

13 17/10/2003 — Telstra Dome

New Zealand: 68	Canada: 6
Tries: Muliaina (4), So'oialo (2), Ralph (2), Meeuws, Nonu	Pens: Barker (2)
Cons: Carter (9)	
15 Leon MacDonald	15 Quentin Fyffe
14 Mils Muliaina	14 Matt King
13 Ma'a Nonu	13 John Cannon
12 Daniel Carter	12 Marco di Girolamo
11 Caleb Ralph	11 Sean Fauth
10 Carlos Spencer	10 Jared Barker
9 Steve Devine	9 Ed Fairhurst
1 Carl Hoeft	1 Kevin Tkachuk
2 Mark Hammett	2 Aaron Abrams
3 Kees Meeuws	3 Garth Cooke
4 Brad Thorn	4 Jamie Cudmore
5 Chris Jack	5 Ed Knaggs
6 Reuben Thorne	6 Ryan Banks
7 Marty Holah	7 Jim Douglas
8 Rodney So'oialo	8 Jeff Reid
16 Corey Flynn*	16 Mark Lawson*
17 Dave Hewett	17 Rod Snow
18 Richie McCaw*	18 Colin Yukes*
19 Daniel Braid*	19 Adam van Staveren*
20 Byron Kelleher	20 Morgan Williams
21 Doug Howlett*	21 Ryan Smith*
22 Greg Somerville	22 Nikyta Witkowski*

Referee Tony Spreadbury

17 19/10/2003 — Canberra Sdm

Wales 27	Tonga 20
Tries: Cooper, M. Williams	Tries: Hola, Lavaka, Kivalu
Cons: S. Jones	Cons: Hola
Pens: S. Jones (4)	Pens: Hola
15 Rhys Williams	15 Sila Va'enuku
14 Mark Jones	14 Sione Fonua
13 Mark Taylor	13 Sukanaivalu Hufanga
12 Iestyn Harris	12 John Payne
11 Tom Shanklin	11 Tevita Tu'ifua
10 Stephen Jones	10 Pierre Hola
9 Gareth Cooper	9 Sililo Martens
1 Iestyn Thomas	1 Kisi Pulu
2 Mefin Davies	2 Viliami Ma'asi
3 Gethin Jenkins	3 Heamani Lavaka
4 Gareth Llewellyn	4 Usaia Latu
5 Robert Sidoli	5 Viliami Vaki
6 Dafydd Jones	6 Ipolito Fenukitau
7 Colin Charvis	7 Stanley Afeaki
8 Alix Popham	8 Benhur Kivalu
16 Huw Bennett*	16 Ephram Taukafa*
17 Adam Jones*	17 Tonga Lea'aetoa*
18 Chris Wyatt*	18 Milton Ngauamo*
19 Martyn Williams*	19 Nisifolo Naufahu*
20 Dwayne Peel*	20 David Palu
21 Shane Williams	21 Sateki Tu'ipulotu
22 Garan Evans	22 Gus Leger

Referee Paul Honiss

21 21/10/2003 — Canberra Sdm

Italy 19	Canada 14
Tries: Parisse	Tries: Fyffe
Cons: Wakarua	Pens: Barker (3)
Pens: Wakarua (4)	
15 Gonzalo Canale	15 Quentin Fyffe
14 Mirco Bergamasco	14 Winston Stanley
13 Cristian Stoica	13 John Cannon
12 Manuel Dallan	12 Marco di Girolamo
11 Denis Dallan	11 Dave Lougheed
10 Rima Wakarua	10 Jared Barker
9 Alessandro Troncon	9 Morgan Williams
1 Andrea Lo Cicero	1 Rod Snow
2 Fabio Ongaro	2 Mark Lawson
3 Martin Castrogiovanni	3 Jon Thiel
4 Santiago Dellape	4 Colin Yukes
5 Marco Bortolami	5 Al Charron
6 Andrea De Rossi	6 Jamie Cudmore
7 Aaron Persico	7 Jim Douglas
8 Sergio Parisse	8 Ryan Banks
16 Carlo Festuccia*	16 Aaron Abrams
17 Salvatore Perugini	17 Kevin Tkachuk*
18 Carlo Checchinato*	18 Jeff Reid
19 Scott Palmer*	19 Josh Jackson*
20 Matteo Mazzantini*	20 Sean Fauth
21 Francesco Mazzariol*	21 Bob Ross
22 Andrea Masi*	22 Matt King

Referee Paddy O'Brien

24 24/10/2003 — Suncorp Stadium

New Zealand 91	Tonga 7
Tries: Ralph (2), Muliaina (2), Howlett (2), Braid, Flynn, Carter, Spencer, Meeuws, MacDonald, pen try	Tries: Hola
Cons: MacDonald (12), Spencer	Cons: Tu'ipulotu
15 Mils Muliaina	15 Sila Va'enuku
14 Doug Howlett	14 Sione Fonua
13 Leon MacDonald	13 Sukanaivalu Hufanga
12 Daniel Carter	12 John Payne
11 Caleb Ralph	11 Tevita Tu'ifua
10 Carlos Spencer	10 Pierre Hola
9 Justin Marshall	9 Sililo Martens
1 Kees Meeuws	1 Kisi Pulu
2 Corey Flynn	2 Viliami Ma'asi
3 Greg Somerville	3 Heamani Lavaka
4 Brad Thorn	4 Usaia Latu
5 Ali Williams	5 Viliami Vaki
6 Reuben Thorne	6 Ipolito Fenukitau
7 Daniel Braid	7 Stanley Afeaki
8 Rodney So'oialo	8 Benhur Kivalu
16 Keven Mealamu	16 Ephram Taukafa*
17 Dave Hewett*	17 Tonga Lea'aetoa*
18 Jerry Collins	18 Milton Ngauamo*
19 Marty Holah*	19 Edward Langi*
20 Richie McCaw*	20 David Palu
21 Ma'a Nonu*	21 Sateki Tu'ipulotu*
22 Ben Atiga*	22 Gus Leger*

Referee Pablo Deluca

27 25/10/2003 — Canberra Sdm

Wales 27	Italy 15
Tries: M. Jones, Parker, Dafydd Jones	Pens: Wakarua (5)
Cons: Harris (3)	
Pens: Harris (2)	
15 Kevin Morgan	15 Gonzalo Canale
14 Mark Jones	14 Nicola Mazzucato
13 Sonny Parker	13 Cristian Stoica
12 Iestyn Harris	12 Andrea Masi
11 Gareth Thomas	11 Denis Dallan
10 Ceri Sweeney	10 Rima Wakarua
9 Dwayne Peel	9 Alessandro Troncon
1 Duncan Jones	1 Andrea Lo Cicero
2 Robin McBryde	2 Fabio Ongaro
3 Adam Jones	3 Martin Castrogiovanni
4 Brent Cockbain	4 Carlo Checchinato
5 Gareth Llewellyn	5 Santiago Dellape
6 Dafydd Jones	6 Andrea De Rossi
7 Martyn Williams	7 Aaron Persico
8 Colin Charvis	8 Sergio Parisse
16 Mefin Davies	16 Carlo Festuccia*
17 Gethin Jenkins*	17 Salvatore Perugini*
18 Robert Sidoli*	18 Matthew Phillips*
19 Jonathan Thomas*	19 Scott Palmer*
20 Gareth Cooper*	20 Mauro Bergamasco*
21 Stephen Jones*	21 Francesco Mazzariol*
22 Rhys Williams*	22 Christian Bezzi*

Referee Andrew Cole

33 29/10/2003 — WIN Stadium

Canada 24	Tonga 7
Tries: Fauth, Abrams	Tries: Afeaki
Cons: Pritchard (2)	Cons: Hola
Pens: Ross (4)	
15 Quentin Fyffe	15 Gus Leger
14 Sean Fauth	14 Pila Fifita
13 Nikyta Witkowski	13 Johnny Ngauamo
12 Marco di Girolamo	12 John Payne
11 Winston Stanley	11 Sione Fonua
10 Bob Ross	10 Pierre Hola
9 Morgan Williams	9 Sililo Martens
1 Rod Snow	1 Tonga Lea'aetoa
2 Mark Lawson	2 Ephram Taukafa
3 Garth Cooke	3 Heamani Lavaka
4 Al Charron	4 Milton Ngauamo
5 Mike James	5 Inoke Afeaki
6 Jamie Cudmore	6 Nisifolo Naufahu
7 Adam van Staveren	7 Sione Tu'Amoheloa
8 Josh Jackson	8 Benhur Kivalu
16 Aaron Abrams*	16 Viliami Ma'asi*
17 Kevin Tkachuk*	17 Kafalosi Tonga*
18 Colin Yukes*	18 Usaia Latu*
19 Jeff Reid*	19 Ipolito Fenukitau*
20 Ed Fairhurst*	20 David Palu*
21 Ryan Smith*	21 Sukanaivalu Hufanga*
22 James Pritchard*	22 Viliami Vaki*

Referee Alain Rolland

40 2/11/2003 — Telstra Stadium

New Zealand 53	Wales 37
Tries: Rocokoko (2), Howlett (2), MacDonald, Williams, Spencer, Mauger	Tries: Taylor, Parker, Charvis, Williams
Cons: MacDonald (5)	Cons: S. Jones (4)
Pens: MacDonald	Pens: S. Jones (3)
15 Mils Muliaina	15 Garan Evans
14 Doug Howlett	14 Shane Williams
13 Leon MacDonald	13 Mark Taylor
12 Aaron Mauger	12 Sonny Parker
11 Joe Rokocoko	11 Tom Shanklin
10 Carlos Spencer	10 Stephen Jones
9 Justin Marshall	9 Gareth Cooper
1 Dave Hewett	1 Iestyn Thomas
2 Keven Mealamu	2 Robin McBryde
3 Greg Somerville	3 Adam Jones
4 Brad Thorn	4 Brent Cockbain
5 Ali Williams	5 Robert Sidoli
6 Reuben Thorne	6 Jonathan Thomas
7 Richie McCaw	7 Colin Charvis
8 Jerry Collins	8 Alix Popham
16 Mark Hammett*	16 Mefin Davies*
17 Kees Meeuws*	17 Gethin Jenkins*
18 Rodney So'oialo*	18 Chris Wyatt*
19 Marty Holah*	19 Dafydd Jones*
20 Byron Kelleher	20 Dwayne Peel*
21 Daniel Carter	21 Ceri Sweeney*
22 Ma'a Nonu	22 Gareth Thomas*

Referee Andre Watson

FINAL POOL TABLE

	W	D	L	F	A	BP	PTS
New Zealand	4	0	0	282	57	4	20
Wales	3	0	1	132	98	2	14
Italy	2	0	2	77	123	0	8
Canada	1	0	3	54	135	1	5
Tonga	0	0	4	46	178	1	1

Quarter-finals

41 8/11/2003 Telstra Dome

New Zealand 29
Tries: MacDonald, Mealamu, Rokocoko
Cons: MacDonald
Pens: MacDonald (3)
DG: Mauger

South Africa 9
Pens: Hougaard (3)

15	Mils Muliaina	15	Jaco vd Westhuyzen
14	Doug Howlett	14	Ashwin Willemse
13	Leon MacDonald	13	Jorrie Muller
12	Aaron Mauger	12	De Wet Barry
11	Joe Rokocoko	11	Thinus Delport
10	Carlos Spencer	10	Derick Hougaard
9	Justin Marshall	9	Joost vd Westhuizen
1	Dave Hewett	1	Christo Bezuidenhout
2	Keven Mealamu	2	John Smit
3	Greg Somerville	3	Faan Rautenbach
4	Chris Jack	4	Bakkies Botha
5	Ali Williams	5	Victor Matfield
6	Reuben Thorne	6	Corne Krige
7	Richie McCaw	7	Danie Rossouw
8	Jerry Collins	8	Juan Smith
16	Mark Hammett*	16	Danie Coetzee*
17	Kees Meeuws*	17	Richard Bands*
18	Brad Thorn*	18	Selborne Boome*
19	Marty Holah*	19	Schalk Burger*
20	Steve Devine*	20	Neil de Kock*
21	Daniel Carter*	21	Louis Koen*
22	Caleb Ralph*	22	Jaque Fourie*

Referee Tony Spreadbury

---

42 8/11/2003 Suncorp Stadium

Australia 33
Tries: Mortlock, Gregan, Lyons
Cons: Flatley (3)
Pens: Flatley (4)

Scotland 16
Tries: Russell
Cons: Paterson
Pens: Paterson (2)
DG: Paterson

15	Mat Rogers	15	Glenn Metcalfe
14	Wendell Sailor	14	Simon Danielli
13	Stirling Mortlock	13	Gregor Townsend
12	Elton Flatley	12	Andrew Henderson
11	Lote Tuqiri	11	Kenny Logan
10	Stephen Larkham	10	Chris Paterson
9	George Gregan	9	Bryan Redpath
1	Bill Young	1	Tom Smith
2	Brendan Cannon	2	Gordon Bulloch
3	Ben Darwin	3	Bruce Douglas
4	Justin Harrison	4	Nathan Hines
5	Nathan Sharpe	5	Stuart Grimes
6	George Smith	6	Jason White
7	Phil Waugh	7	Cameron Mather
8	David Lyons	8	Simon Taylor
16	Jeremy Paul*	16	Rob Russell*
17	Al Baxter*	17	Gordon McIlwham*
18	Daniel Vickerman*	18	Scott Murray*
19	Matt Cockbain*	19	Jon Petrie*
20	Chris Whitaker*	20	Michael Blair*
21	Matt Giteau*	21	James McLaren*
22	Joe Roff*	22	Ben Hinshelwood*

Referee Steve Walsh

---

43 9/11/2003 Telstra Dome

France 43
Tries: Magne, Dominici, Harinordoquy, Crenca
Cons: Michalak (4)
Pens: Michalak (5)

Ireland 21
Tries: Maggs, O'Driscoll (2)
Cons: Humphreys (3)

15	Nicolas Brusque	15	Girvan Dempsey
14	Aurelien Rougerie	14	Shane Horgan
13	Tony Marsh	13	Brian O'Driscoll
12	Yannick Jauzion	12	Kevin Maggs
11	Christophe Dominici	11	John Kelly
10	Frederic Michalak	10	Ronan O'Gara
9	Fabien Galthie	9	Peter Stringer
1	Jean Jacques Crenca	1	Reggie Corrigan
2	Raphael Ibanez	2	Keith Wood
3	Sylvain Marconnet	3	John Hayes
4	Fabien Pelous	4	Malcolm O'Kelly
5	Jerome Thion	5	Paul O'Connell
6	Serge Betsen	6	Simon Easterby
7	Olivier Magne	7	Keith Gleeson
8	Imanol Harinordoquy	8	Victor Costello
16	Yannick Bru*	16	Shane Byrne*
17	Olivier Milloud*	17	Marcus Horan*
18	Olivier Brouzet*	18	D. O'Callaghan*
19	Patrick Tabacco*	19	Eric Miller*
20	Gerald Merceron	20	Guy Easterby*
21	Brian Liebenberg*	21	David Humphreys*
22	Pepito Elhorga*	22	Anthony Horgan

Referee Jonathan Kaplan

---

44 9/11/2003 Suncorp Stadium

England 28
Tries: Greenwood
Cons: Wilkinson
Pens: Wilkinson (6)
DG: Wilkinson

Wales 17
Tries: S. Jones, Charvis, M. Williams
Cons: Harris

15	Jason Robinson	15	Gareth Thomas
14	Dan Luger	14	Mark Jones
13	Will Greenwood	13	Mark Taylor
12	Mike Tindall	12	Iestyn Harris
11	Ben Cohen	11	Shane Williams
10	Jonny Wilkinson	10	Stephen Jones
9	Matt Dawson	9	Gareth Cooper
1	Jason Leonard	1	Iestyn Thomas
2	Steve Thompson	2	Robin McBryde
3	Phil Vickery	3	Adam Jones
4	Martin Johnson	4	Brent Cockbain
5	Ben Kay	5	Robert Sidoli
6	Lewis Moody	6	Dafydd Jones
7	Neil Back	7	Colin Charvis
8	Lawrence Dallaglio	8	Jonathan Thomas
16	Dorian West	16	Mefin Davies*
17	Trevor Woodman*	17	Gethin Jenkins*
18	Simon Shaw	18	Gareth Llewellyn*
19	Joe Worsley	19	Martyn Williams*
20	Kyran Bracken*	20	Dwayne Peel*
21	Mike Catt*	21	Ceri Sweeney*
22	Stuart Abbott*	22	Kevin Morgan*

Referee Alain Rolland

Semi-finals

45 15/11/2003 Telstra Stadium

New Zealand 10
Tries: Thorne
Cons: MacDonald
Pens: MacDonald

Australia 22
Tries: Mortlock
Cons: Flatley
Pens: Flatley (5)

15	Mils Muliaina	15	Mat Rogers
14	Doug Howlett	14	Wendell Sailor
13	Leon MacDonald	13	Stirling Mortlock
12	Aaron Mauger	12	Elton Flatley
11	Joe Rokocoko	11	Lote Tuqiri
10	Carlos Spencer	10	Stephen Larkham
9	Justin Marshall	9	George Gregan
1	Dave Hewett	1	Bill Young
2	Keven Mealamu	2	Brendan Cannon
3	Greg Somerville	3	Ben Darwin
4	Chris Jack	4	Justin Harrison
5	Ali Williams	5	Nathan Sharpe
6	Reuben Thorne	6	George Smith
7	Richie McCaw	7	Phil Waugh
8	Jerry Collins	8	David Lyons
16	Mark Hammett	16	Jeremy Paul*
17	Kees Meeuws*	17	Al Baxter*
18	Brad Thorn*	18	David Giffin*
19	Marty Holah*	19	Matt Cockbain*
21	Daniel Carter	20	Chris Whitaker
22	Caleb Ralph	21	Nathan Grey*
		22	Joe Roff*

Referee Chris White

---

46 16/11/2003 Telstra Stadium

France 7
Tries: Betsen
Cons: Michalak

England 24
Pens: Wilkinson (5)
DG: Wilkinson (3)

15	Nicolas Brusque	15	Josh Lewsey
14	Aurelien Rougerie	14	Jason Robinson
13	Tony Marsh	13	Will Greenwood
12	Yannick Jauzion	12	Mike Catt
11	Christophe Dominici	11	Ben Cohen
10	Frederic Michalak	10	Jonny Wilkinson
9	Fabien Galthie	9	Matt Dawson
1	Jean Jacques Crenca	1	Trevor Woodman
2	Raphael Ibanez	2	Steve Thompson
3	Sylvain Marconnet	3	Phil Vickery
4	Fabien Pelous	4	Martin Johnson
5	Jerome Thion	5	Ben Kay
6	Serge Betsen	6	Richard Hill
7	Olivier Magne	7	Neil Back
8	Imanol Harinordoquy	8	Lawrence Dallaglio
16	Yannick Bru	16	Dorian West*
17	Olivier Milloud*	17	Jason Leonard*
18	David Auradou	18	Martin Corry
19	Christian Labit*	19	Lewis Moody*
20	Gerald Merceron*	20	Kyran Bracken*
21	Damien Traille	21	Mike Tindall*
22	Clement Poitrenaud*	22	Iain Balshaw

Referee Paddy O'Brien

3rd/4th Play-off

47 20/11/2003 Telstra Stadium   NEW ZEALAND   FRANCE

New Zealand 40
Tries: Jack, Howlett, Rokocoko, Thorn, Muliaina, Holah
Cons: MacDonald, Carter (4)

France 13
Tries: Elhorga
Cons: Yachvili
Pens: Yachvili
DG: Yachvili

15	Mils Muliaina	15	Clement Poitrenaud
14	Doug Howlett	14	Pepito Elhorga
13	Leon MacDonald	13	Tony Marsh
12	Aaron Mauger	12	Damien Traille
11	Joe Rokocoko	11	David Bory
10	Carlos Spencer	10	Gerald Merceron
9	Steve Devine	9	Dmitri Yachvili
1	Dave Hewett	1	Sylvain Marconnet
2	Keven Mealamu	2	Yannick Bru
3	Greg Somerville	3	Jean Baptiste Poux
4	Chris Jack	4	David Auradou
5	Ali Williams	5	Thibault Privat
6	Reuben Thorne	6	Sebastien Chabal
7	Richie McCaw	7	Patrick Tabacco
8	Jerry Collins	8	Christian Labit
16	Mark Hammett*	16	Raphael Ibanez*
17	Carl Hoeft*	17	Jean Jacques Crenca*
18	Brad Thorn*	18	Fabien Pelous*
19	Marty Holah*	19	Olivier Magne*
20	Byron Kelleher	20	Frederic Michalak*
21	Daniel Carter*	21	Brian Liebenberg*
22	Caleb Ralph*	22	Nicolas Brusque*

Referee Chris White

RUGBY WORLD CUP 2003 – The Final

48 22/11/2003 Telstra Stadium   AUSTRALIA   ENGLAND

Australia 17
(after extra time)
Tries: Tuqiri
Pens: Flatley (4)

England 20
Tries: Robinson
Pens: Wilkinson (4)
DG: Wilkinson

15	Mat Rogers	15	Josh Lewsey
14	Wendell Sailor	14	Jason Robinson
13	Stirling Mortlock	13	Will Greenwood
12	Elton Flatley	12	Mike Tindall
11	Lote Tuqiri	11	Ben Cohen
10	Stephen Larkham	10	Jonny Wilkinson
9	George Gregan	9	Matt Dawson
1	Bill Young	1	Trevor Woodman
2	Brendan Cannon	2	Steve Thompson
3	Al Baxter	3	Phil Vickery
4	Justin Harrison	4	Martin Johnson
5	Nathan Sharpe	5	Ben Kay
6	George Smith	6	Richard Hill
7	Phil Waugh	7	Neil Back
8	David Lyons	8	Lawrence Dallaglio
16	Jeremy Paul*	16	Dorian West
17	Matt Dunning*	17	Jason Leonard*
18	David Giffin*	18	Martin Corry
19	Matt Cockbain*	19	Lewis Moody*
20	Chris Whitaker	20	Kyran Bracken
21	Matt Giteau*	21	Mike Catt*
22	Joe Roff*	22	Iain Balshaw*

Referee Andre Watson